THE BATTLE
OF
PLATTE
BRIDGE

.

By J. W. Vaughn

.

UNIVERSITY OF OKLAHOMA PRESS : NORMAN

By J. W. Vaughn

With Crook at the Rosebud (Harrisburg, Pa., 1956)
The Reynolds Campaign on Powder River (Norman, 1961)
The Battle of Platte Bridge (Norman, 1963)

LIBRARY OF CONGRESS CATALOG CARD NUMBER: 64-11316

Copyright 1963 by the University of Oklahoma Press, Publishing Division of the University. Composed and printed at Norman, Oklahoma, U.S.A., by the University of Oklahoma Press. First edition.

Dedicated to the memory of the late L. C. Bishop,
who collaborated in this research

Preface

THIS IS THE STORY of the battle between troopers of the Eleventh Kansas Cavalry and hostile Sioux, Cheyenne, and Arapaho Indians at Platte Bridge Station, near the present site of Casper, Wyoming, on July 25 and 26, 1865. The combined tribes had declared war against the white man in retaliation for the heavy losses inflicted upon them the previous year by the army under General Sully at Killdeer Mountain, Dakota Territory, and the destruction of the village of Southern Cheyennes at Sand Creek in eastern Colorado. The warriors from the large encampment in the Powder River country laid siege to the garrison at Platte Bridge Station with the avowed purpose of destroying this important post guarding the Oregon Trail.

After some skirmishing, a detachment was sent out from the fort in the morning under Lieutenant Caspar Collins to bring in a small wagon train expected to arrive from Sweetwater Station, fifty miles to the west. After going about a mile, the detachment rode into an ambush and barely cut its way back to the fort, with the loss of Lieutenant Collins and four other men.

About noon the wagon train was sighted coming over the divide west of the post. It was immediately surrounded and attacked by the warriors. After one of the most vicious little fights in our history, the twenty men in the supply train were killed and the wagons burned. The battle lasted four hours, and the Indians suffered such severe losses that they abandoned the siege and returned to their home lodges.

This is a highly detailed and factual reconstruction of these dramatic encounters which saw the young and gallant Caspar Collins fall while protecting the rear of his retreating detachment and an obscure commissary sergeant named Amos J. Custard gallantly lead his doomed little band in the supply train to death and glory.

The author is indebted to a number of Casper residents for aid in this research. Marion N. Wheeler, assisted by the late Albert M. Zuill, prepared accurate sketches of the battlefield area. W. G. and Connie Boles lent every facility and encouragement in the exploration of the Custard site on their ranch. Mark J. Davis and other members of the Fort Caspar Commission were helpful in many ways.

James S. Hutchins of McLean, Virginia, a well-known authority on army equipment and transportation, has graciously furnished photographs and technical information.

Alberta Pantle, librarian of the Kansas Historical Society, has provided an extensive bibliography and other material from the files of the Society. J. B. Dodson of Manhattan, Kansas, and Frank Sibrava of Wilson, Kansas, have given freely of their time in searching for new material.

Elsie Price and John T. W. Price, granddaughter and great-grandson of Sergeant Custard; Ethel D. Truit, daughter of Lieutenant George Drew; and Victoria Shrader, daughter of Corporal James W. Shrader, have furnished photographs and biographical data.

I am grateful to my wife, Florence, for accompanying me on the field trips and for providing the creature comforts which are so necessary.

J. W. VAUGHN

Windsor, Colorado
January 10, 1964

Contents and Illustrations

ILLUSTRATIONS

The Battle of Platte Bridge

Ft. Laramie
July 27, 1865

MAJ. J. W. BARNES, *Asst Adjutant Gen*

One thousand Indians attacked Platte Station on Tuesday; been fighting two days. Lt Collins 11th Ohio Cav. and 25 men, 11th Kansas Cav. killed, 9 wounded. Bodies scalped and horribly mutilated. . . . They are now 3 miles west destroying telegraph line. The left column is now en route there; the balance will leave in two days. I start for Platte Bridge myself Saturday. I respectfully ask something be done to hurry contractors. Ammunition transferred to contractors months since, and of which I am short, has not arrived. I start on my expedition with scant supply of stores and many bare-footed horses.

P. E. CONNOR
Brig. Gen.

(U. S. Serial Set [U. S. Congress], Serial 3436, *H. R. Doc.* 369, Pt. 1, p. 357)

The Eleventh Kansas Cavalry

WHEN THE UNION ARMY under General McClellan was thrown back from Richmond in the summer of 1862, President Lincoln issued a call for more troops. It was a time of great gloom and despondency in the North, as it was apparent that the Civil War would be long and drawn out. The state of Kansas had already furnished ten regiments for the Union Army from its sparse population and was now called upon to furnish three more. The counties had been stripped of all foot-loose men, of all who could reasonably be called upon to go to the field. There remained only the men of families, farmers and mechanics, all poor and just getting a firm foothold in the state of their adoption. Still suffering from the drouth and famine of 1860, "Bleeding Kansas" was beset on the east and south by border ruffians and guerrilla bands and the ever present threat of the Confederate Army, and on the west and north by unfriendly Indians. The Eleventh Kansas regiment of ten companies under the command of Colonel Thomas Ewing, Lieutenant Colonel Moonlight, and Major Preston B. Plumb,[1] was promptly recruited within a month. It was composed of a strange mixture of teen-age boys and older family men. Nothing but the imminent peril of the Republic and the immediate necessity for more men in its defense

[1] For complete life history see W. E. Connelley, *The Life of Preston B. Plumb.*

3

could have justified the latter in forsaking their dependent families. They knew that their enlistment bounties of one hundred dollars and their army pay would be slow in coming. No history will record the heroic struggles of these men at the recruiting stations when they resolved to leave their ill-provided families for the hazards of three years of distant service.[2]

Company H was organized by Captain Joel Huntoon in August, 1862, at Tecumseh, Kansas, near Topeka, and was composed mostly of men from Shawnee County in the eastern part of the state. After a march of fifty miles the company arrived at Camp Lyon, the regimental rendezvous near Fort Leavenworth, on September 7, and was mustered into the United States Army one week later.[3]

Company D was recruited by Captain Peleg Thomas from the neighboring counties of Leavenworth, Jefferson, and Osage, and was mustered in at Camp Lyon on September 13.[4]

The regiment had not even been fully armed and equipped before it was called upon to go by forced marches to join other Union troops to meet the Confederate forces advancing in Arkansas. After a series of rapid marches as infantry, during which the men suffered many hardships, they arrived in time to take part in the vicious little battles of Cane Hill, Arkansas, on December 6, and Prairie Grove, Arkansas, on the following day.[5] At Cane Hill, Company H reinforced the pickets and had a desperate struggle at the summit of a mountain, but, after a brave stand, was pushed back by the overwhelming numbers of the enemy. Although the company lost many men in the vain effort to hold the summit, its members gained the reputation of

2 "Military History of the Eleventh Kansas Volunteer Cavalry," *Report of the Adjutant General of the State of Kansas, 1861–1865,* 200, 215; Andreas, *History of the State of Kansas,* 195–96.

3 Muster Roll of Company H, 11th Kansas Cavalry, August 31, 1865.

4 Muster Roll of Company D, 11th Kansas Cavalry, August 31, 1865.

5 Complete descriptions with maps of all Civil War engagements in which the Eleventh Kansas Cavalry participated are contained in Connelley, *The Life of Preston B. Plumb.*

being brave fighters. Company D also distinguished itself in the center of the line and was the last off the field. Prairie Grove was one of the bloodiest, and by far the most decisive, of battles fought in Arkansas during the Civil War. The Confederates were driven back and retreated over the Arkansas River, while the Eleventh Kansas returned to Springfield, Missouri, to spend the winter. Many men were lost as the result of sickness and disease incurred during the severe weather. The next spring the regiment marched to Kansas City, where it arrived April 20, 1863. As it had lost three hundred men, it was recruited up to full strength. The men were mounted, since horses had been obtained, and the outfit now qualified as a cavalry regiment.[6]

For the next year the men did border service, which consisted of fighting bushwhackers, escorting trains, and scouting in Missouri and Kansas. They clashed with Quantrill's guerrillas at Sibley, Missouri, on August 14, 1863, and at Lawrence, Kansas, on August 21, 1863, driving them back into Missouri. The recruiting of Companies L and M brought the regimental strength up to twelve companies.[7]

On October 12, 1864, the regiment rendezvoused to meet the invasion of Missouri by the Confederate General Price. It met the enemy at Lexington, Missouri, on October 19 and, after driving them from that place, engaged in a series of skirmishes at Little Blue. Here the regiment fought a delaying action to cover the retreat of other Union troops to Lexington. Company H held an important ford until late in the day, saving much of the right flank. The Union troops rallied and drove the enemy southward along the state line in a series of engagements at Westport, Cold Water Grove, Mound City, and Fort Lincoln. The Eleventh Kansas pursued the rebels from Fort Scott and drove them across the Arkansas River, thus ending the threat. The regiment returned to Kansas, arriving at Paola on Decem-

---

[6] "Military History of the Eleventh Kansas Volunteer Cavalry," *loc. cit.,* 205.
[7] *Ibid.,* 206

ber 12. It had always been assigned to the most difficult and dangerous duties—in the advance on offensive movements and to the rear during retreat, showing the reliance placed upon it.[8]

As an expedition was being organized by General Connor to attack the hostile Indians in the Powder River country, Companies A, B, D, F, H, I, K, L, and M of the Eleventh Kansas Cavalry were soon ordered to Fort Riley to recruit and refit for service on the plains. Company D, which had not served in the Price campaign, rejoined the regiment at this time. There was a shortage of horses and supplies, these being needed in the more important operations in the east, so that one-third of the regiment remained dismounted. On February 20, 1865, the march was commenced for Fort Kearny, Nebraska, where the men arrived on March 4, after a difficult march during which it was necessary to rebuild the bridges in order to cross the swollen streams. During the two days' halt at Fort Kearny supplies were drawn, horses shod, and equipment repaired.[9]

The column reached Fort Laramie on April 9, when news was received of Lee's surrender. The men celebrated the victory that night and did many foolish things, none getting any sleep. Since General Connor had decided not to use the regiment in his Powder River expedition, he detached it for service in guarding the telegraph line and the emigrant roads and for preventing the Indians from going south across the North Platte River. The march was continued westward along the Oregon Trail. At the telegraph station at Deer Creek on April 18, news was received of the assassination of President Lincoln. When they heard this, the men were very angry. Some wept; some were angry beyond all reason, demanding of their officers that they go south and clean out the whole country.[10]

[8] *Ibid.*, 207

[9] *Ibid.*, 208; Andreas *op. cit.*, 196; S. H. Fairfield, "The Eleventh Kansas Regiment at Platte Bridge," *Kansas Historical Collections*, VIII, 353.

[10] Charles Waring, "The Platte Bridge Battle," Riley County *Democrat*, August 26, 1909.

The next day the regiment marched twenty-eight miles west to Platte Station, which was also called "Platte Bridge" or "Platte Bridge Station," leaving Major Adams in command of Companies D and L at Deer Creek Station. Preston B. Plumb, who had been promoted to lieutenant colonel of the regiment when Thomas Moonlight was made a full colonel, set up regimental headquarters at Camp Dodge, four miles to the southeast of Platte Station on the east side of upper Garden Creek, where there was plenty of wood and water.

Lieutenant Henry C. Bretney (later Captain Bretney), who had been in command of Company G, Eleventh Ohio Cavalry, ever since the death of Captain L. M. Rinehart, had his headquarters at Platte Station, while detachments of his company occupied block stations about fifty miles apart to the west, the first being Sweetwater Station; the second, Three Crossings of the Sweetwater; the third, Rocky Ridge, also known as St. Mary's; and the fourth, Pacific Springs on South Pass. Captain Greer, with Company I, and Captain Joel Huntoon, with Company H, were sent on to Sweetwater Station, fifty-two miles west of Platte Station, while detachments from these companies occupied stations farther west, including Rocky Ridge and Three Crossings.[11] The regiment was thus divided up so as to reinforce three companies of the Eleventh Ohio Cavalry and two companies of the Third U. S. Volunteers, which were guarding the whole telegraph route along the Oregon Trail from Fort Laramie to South Pass, nearly three hundred miles. There was a shortage of supplies and ammunition. The troops were almost totally dismounted, since Indian raids along the route had stampeded most of their horses.[12]

[11] George M. Walker, "Eleventh Kansas Cavalry, 1865, and the Battle of Platte Bridge," *Kansas Historical Collections,* XIV 334; Isaac B. Pennock, "Diary," *Annals of Wyoming,* Vol. XXIII (July, 1951), 5–6.

All quoted material in this work has been copied without alteration from the original sources. Errors in grammar, punctuation, and spelling occur so frequently that no attempt has been made to edit or correct them.

[12] "Military History of the Eleventh Kansas Volunteer Cavalry," *loc. cit.,* 209.

Old Platte Bridge Station was located on the south side of the North Platte River about 130 miles west of Fort Laramie and at the western edge of the present city of Casper, Wyoming. The station was a stockade inside of which were accommodations for a garrison of one hundred men. North of the station a few yards was the bridge, one thousand feet long and thirteen feet wide. The station was at a junction of the three main branches of the Oregon Trail coming in from the east—two on the north side of the river and the telegraph road on the south side. After crossing the bridge from the station, the telegraph road ran along the bottomland and then, after angling up the bluff, joined the branch north of the river which ran westward along the low bluff in plain sight of the station. About one mile west the road ran up into some sand hills, which formed a low divide, and then down into flat country until it ascended again to cross between two mounds forming a saddle in another, higher divide four miles west of the station. The telegraph line ran along the south side of this road. The south branch of the Oregon Trail continued westward south of the river, while the third branch ran past the bridge about a mile to the north. Two miles west of the fort the telegraph road ran close to a bend of the river, where there was a popular camping place. From here there extended a short cut to the fort running eastward along the bottomland, so that it was possible to go there without following the telegraph line, which went up over the divide. The country north of the river was covered with sand hills and deep ravines.[13]

From 1840 to 1847 the site of the station was known as "Camp Platte." Since it was a convenient and natural camping place on the Oregon Road, many travelers stopped here for a day or two to rest and prepare for the long journey ahead. In June, 1847, the Mormons established a ferry here for their own use, and the

[13] Material on the Oregon Trail in this work is taken from maps and data furnished by L. C. Bishop, a well-known authority on the subject, and from personal reconnaissance.

8

place was called "Mormon Ferry" until a bridge was built in 1859. The military post, first built here in the summer of 1858, was occupied by soldiers on July 29 "to keep open communication with Salt Lake City and to aid prompt forwarding of supplies." The first troops stationed here were Companies D and E, Fourth Artillery, under the command of Captain Joseph Roberts and Captain G. W. Getty, who were part of the second column of the Utah expedition. The fort buildings, of sun-dried bricks, were crude and small. The soldiers were withdrawn in 1859.[14]

The first bridge in the area was built of logs in 1854–55 by John Richaud, Sr. (also spelled "Richard" or "Reshaw"), a Frenchman from St. Charles, Missouri, at a ford near the present Evansville, Wyoming, seven miles down the river from the crossing where Platte Bridge was later built. As this was the only bridge in the vicinity from 1855 to 1859, Richaud did a profitable business. When the river was high in the spring and summer, he usually charged five dollars for a team and wagon to cross his bridge. If the stream was low so that the emigrants might take a chance in swimming their animals across, Richaud would reduce the price to three dollars and sometimes would charge only two dollars. From fifty cents to one dollar was the charge for each person and for each animal not included with the team hitched to the wagon. Richaud generally received gold as his toll but sometimes accepted furniture and other household necessities from emigrants who had overloaded their wagons when they started from the East. He had a cabin, a blacksmith shop, and a few other buildings on the south side of the river.[15] A little community grew up here; and as one or two detachments of soldiers had been stationed there temporarily, it was sometimes called "Richaud's Post" or "Camp Payne."[16]

[14] Alfred J. Mokler, *History of Natrona County,* 449; Alfred J. Mokler, *Fort Caspar,* 10.

[15] Mokler, *History of Natrona County,* 109, 110, 448, 449 .

[16] Robert Ellison, "The Platte Bridge Fight," *Winners of the West,* Vol. III (March 15, 1926), 6–7.

Richaud was married to a Sioux woman and had five or six children. During the season, the bridge was tended by his sons, John Richaud, Jr., and Louis Richaud, who were assisted one summer by young Baptiste Pourrier, better known as "Big Bat," who had just come out from St. Charles to work for John Richaud, Sr. Pourrier married a daughter of his employer and later became famous as a scout for General Crook in his expeditions against the hostile Sioux and Cheyennes. He and Louis Richaud were close friends, the latter serving General Crook as a guide and Sioux interpreter.[17] The widow of Big Bat, who at the time lived on the Pine Ridge Reservation, visited Casper in 1918 and, in company with James H. Bury, visited the spot where the old bridge had spanned the river and pointed out where their cabin, blacksmith shop, and other buildings had been located.[18] John Richaud, Sr., was an enterprising person who carried on an extensive trade with the Indians and furnished wood and hay to the forts under contract, using his sons and Big Bat as employees. During the winter months when the bridge was not in use, he retired to his ranch on Reshaw Creek near its confluence with Chugwater Creek.[19] When the bridge was burned by the Indians in 1867, he moved his family to the French-Indian settlements below Fort Laramie. In 1875 Richaud and Al Palladie were shot

[17] Eli S. Ricker, "Life of Big Bat as Told by Himself," Interviews (MS in Nebraska State Historical Society), Tablet 15, p. 75 ff.

[18] Mokler, *History of Natrona County*, 110.

In November, 1962, a short distance northeast of Evansville, heavy earthmoving equipment uncovered the unmarked graves of seven persons who had been buried in the early days near the Richaud settlement. On a small knoll a half-mile south of the North Platte River, there were the remains of five men, one woman, and one Indian. Four of the men had been buried in military uniforms. It is speculated that these may have been washed down the river from the original burial site opposite Platte Station, as the well-made caskets were filled with sediment.

This discovery inspired further exploration, and the rocky piers of the old Richaud Bridge were soon found, together with the sites of the blacksmith shop and the trading post. See Casper (Wyoming) *Star-Tribune*, Annual Wyoming Edition (March 10, 1963).

[19] Ricker, *loc. cit.*, 75 ff.

and killed at Running Water Crossing, between the Red Cloud Agency and Fort Laramie. Richaud was said to have had a considerable amount of money with him. Suspicion pointed to a man known as "California Joe" as the murderer, and the Indian relatives of Richaud were not long in avenging the death of the two men by killing him.[20]

About the same time that Richaud built his bridge, Louis Guinard built and operated a toll bridge across the Sweetwater River below Independence Rock. In the fall of 1857 and spring of 1858 he built north of the Mormon Ferry a substantial one-thousand-foot span bridge of hewn pine and cottonwood logs supported by twenty-eight piers, thirty feet from center to center, built up in the river of pine logs filled with rocks. He was assisted by his brother, two nephews and one Martin Oliver, who lived in Casper for many years later. Guinard lived with a Shoshoni woman and her two half-blood nephews. The original cost of the bridge was $30,000, but each year more was spent on the building of new piers and other structural work. The total cost was estimated at $60,000. He charged from one to six dollars for the crossing of a six-mule team over his bridge, according to the state of the river. Upon completion of the bridge, the name of the crossing was changed to Platte Bridge Station.[21]

In order to maintain the telegraph line, which now ran from coast to coast, and to serve as escorts for emigrant trains, troops reoccupied the post at Platte Bridge in May, 1862. A log building twelve feet wide by thirty-two feet long was built a short distance southwest of the bridge as a telegraph office and accommodations for the telegrapher. Early in the spring of 1865, on the recommendation of Colonel William O. Collins, the post was changed "from an occasional troop station to a permanent fort, consisting of stores, a blacksmith shop, telegraph station, and

---

[20] Mokler, *History of Natrona County*, 110.

[21] Mokler, *Fort Caspar*, 9, 10, 11, 12; Agnes Wright Spring, *Caspar Collins*, 79–80.

other buildings sufficient to garrison about 100 men." The soldiers occupied the adobe buildings and in the spring of 1865 built a storeroom for supplies. A log store building, operated by Guinard, stood a short distance southeast of the bridge.[22]

The adobe buildings formed three sides of a square, while a stockade providing stabling for about fifty horses formed the other side. The stockade, which enclosed all the buildings except the store and the storeroom, was made of logs rising twelve feet above the ground, so that Indians could not shoot the horses. The adobe buildings faced inside onto the courtyard. The post was believed by Colonel Collins to be defensible by a howitzer and twenty men.[23]

By order of the War Department dated November 21, 1865, the post was designated "Fort Casper" in honor of Lieutenant Caspar W. Collins, who had been killed there in the fighting of July 26, 1865.[24] Through some error the Lieutenant's name was spelled "Casper" in the order, and this spelling was adopted for the name of the city which later grew up near the post.

Fort Casper was promptly burned by the Indians when the army abandoned the post on October 19, 1867. At the same time the bridge located there and Richaud's bridge seven miles to the east were also burned, and the country was abandoned to the Indians for the next ten years.[25]

Platte Bridge was a strategic point—the last crossing for the heavy travel coming up the south branch of the Oregon Trail. Since the main emigrant trains and gold-seekers continued to use all the branches of the old road, it was necessary to protect this travel and maintain the telegraph line. The Indians from the Powder River country crossed here on their forays to the southern Overland route, where they reaped a rich harvest

---

[22] Mokler, *Fort Caspar,* 13, 15, 55.

[23] *Ibid.,* 15, 51, 55; Spring, *op. cit.,* 79–80.

[24] C. G. Coutant, *The History of Wyoming,* 478.

[25] Mokler, *Fort Caspar,* 56; Mokler, *History of Natrona County,* 110, 112, 405.

12

plundering and robbing richly laden trains, the U. S. mail, and valuable express. Since the soldiers at the bridge were a hindrance to their predatory raids, the tribes had determined to destroy the post at the first opportunity. The station was a dangerous one for the soldiers, as the Indians were always running off stock, attacking isolated parties of soldiers, and cutting the telegraph wire.[26]

[26] Mokler, *Fort Caspar,* 17; Spring, *op. cit.,* 76–78; Andreas, *op. cit.,* 196; "Military History of the Eleventh Kansas Volunteer Cavalry," *loc. cit.,* 210.

2

Guidons on the Oregon Trail

THE KANSAS TROOPS had no sooner been distributed to the little frontier posts from Fort Laramie to South Pass than they were called into action. The Indians swarmed along the telegraph line and there were frequent clashes with the soldiers. A few days after their arrival at Platte Station, dispatches were received from Captain Marshall, commanding Company E of the Eleventh Ohio Cavalry, at La Bonté Station, advising that Indians had stampeded all of his horses and asking that a force be sent in pursuit. Companies D and L were sent from Deer Creek Station, twenty-eight miles east of Platte Station, but the horses were not recovered. At this time the soldiers were ignorant of Indian fighting and, after their successes during the Civil War held the warriors in contempt.[1]

Detachments of Companies H and I were surrounded by three hundred to five hundred Indians at Three Crossings Station on May 20 but held out until ninety men arrived as reinforcements from Sweetwater Station.[2] On the same day Indians attacked Deer Creek Station. Although seven of them were killed, Colonel Plumb failed to recover the twenty-six cavalry

[1] "Military History of the Eleventh Kansas Volunteer Cavalry," *loc. cit.*, 209–10.

[2] Pennock, *loc. cit.*, 6.

horses which had been stolen. A man of Company A of the Eleventh Kansas Cavalry was killed and several horses injured during the skirmish.[3] The mules were stampeded at Platte Station on May 24, the Indians capturing forty of them. The herd guards were strengthened to ten men, while two noncoms and six men from each squadron served as night guards.[4]

On May 25, Company I was moved from Sweetwater Station to the regimental headquarters at Camp Dodge, while Company H marched to Platte Station. Rocky Ridge Station, far to the west, was attacked by a strong force on May 27 and burned on June 1.[5]

On June 3, Indians appeared on the bank north of Platte Bridge, and a messenger was sent to Colonel Plumb at Camp Dodge. The Colonel, with ten men of Company G, Eleventh Ohio Cavalry, and some men of Companies A and F of the Eleventh Kansas Cavalry, chased the Indians for about five miles, when the latter suddenly doubled back in an effort to cut off the men. This maneuver failed when relief parties were seen coming up. Some of the soldiers pursued the Indians, but their horses were not in good condition and could not catch the fleet little ponies. In this engagement Private William T. Bonwell of Company F, Eleventh Kansas Cavalry, and Private Tilman Stahlnecker of Company G, Eleventh Ohio Cavalry, were killed, and a number of cavalry horses shot. Bonwell got some distance in advance and the Indians turned on him. As his horse was shot, he was dismounted and unable to get away. When found, he had ten arrows shot into him and was scalped and terribly mangled, with all of his fingers cut off. The soldiers buried him where he fell, about five miles southwest of Casper, and erected a monument over the remains.[6]

---

[3] *Ibid.*

[4] *Ibid.*

[5] *Ibid.*, 7–8; Spring, *op. cit.*, 75–76; Coutant, *op. cit.*, 448. The latter contains the official report of Lieutenant Colonel Preston B. Plumb of this engagement.

[6] Pennock, *loc. cit.*, 8; Spring, *op. cit.*, 77; Robert B. David, *Finn Burnett,*

By the middle of June many stations on the heavily traveled Overland route to the south had been burned and the stage horses driven off. All travel had stopped. On June 11, General Connor ordered Colonel Plumb to take Companies A, B, F, L, and M of his regiment, proceed to Fort Halleck, and reopen the southern route. Colonel Plumb arrived at Fort Halleck on the twenty-fourth of June and at once distributed troops from Fort Collins, Colorado Territory, to Green River, Wyoming, a distance of about four hundred miles. For two hundred miles along this route the Indians had driven off all the stage horses. Plumb had to use his cavalry horses to haul coaches; and as the drivers had left the line because of the danger, soldiers were detailed as drivers. The distance to be protected was so large and the troops so few in number that large escorts for the coaches could not be furnished, ten men being the maximum force at any station.[7]

On July 1, when Indians attacked an emigrant train of one hundred wagons with families at Rock Creek, on the southern route, a detachment of twenty-one men of L Company rescued the train and drove off the Indians. On July 4 a detachment of Companies A and L had a brush with Indians near Fort Halleck, in which Sergeant Gale of Company A was killed. The Indian attacks were successfully met along this route, and the stage lines were maintained all through the difficulties. These five companies were kept busy on scout duty until relieved in August, when they started back to Fort Leavenworth for muster-out service.[8]

At the same time that Colonel Plumb took five companies to the Fort Halleck route, Companies D and H were moved farther east on the Oregon Trail to La Bonté Station and Horseshoe Sta-

---

Frontiersman, 52–56. Toward the end of the century, the remains of Private Bonwell were moved to the Fort D. A. Russell cemetery, where they are buried in Section C, No. 233.

[7] "Military History of the Eleventh Kansas Volunteer Cavalry," *loc. cit.,* 211.

[8] *Ibid.;* Walker, *loc. cit.,* 335.

tion.[9] According to its muster roll, Company K moved from La Prelle Creek thirty miles westward to Deer Creek on July 11. On June 28 the regimental headquarters, which included the band and hospital staff—about thirty men in all—was moved to La Bonté Station, and Company I went to Platte Bridge.[10]

On June 22, First Sergeant Albert L. Rivers of Company D wrote a letter from Camp Horseshoe which was published in the July 8 issue of the Oskaloosa (Kansas) *Independent*:

> FRIEND ROBERTS—Trouble with the Indians seems to be on the increase. Scarcely a day passes but what we hear of some depredations being committed by them, and thus far they seem to have the best of it. . . .
>
> A member of Co. A, 11th Kansas, named Silas Henshaw was killed at Deer Creek on the 17th. He had left camp about 200 yards to get some wood, when three Indians suddenly attacked him. He emptied his revolver at them, badly wounding one, when he was struck with three arrows, inflicting wounds which caused his death the next day.
>
> The Road is closely watched by Indians, and they let no opportunity pass of attacking stragglers from a command, or any small train poorly escorted. This will cause emigration to be very light this season. The telegraph operator at Sweetwater station was killed on the 21st by Indians. He had gone out with ten men to repair the wire which had been broken, when a party of Indians attacked them, killing the operator, and wounding one of the soldiers.
>
> Four companies of the 11th were sent over the Southern Route this week. The Indians have stampeded the herds of several trains, which are laid up, unable to proceed.
>
> Yours,
>
> A. L. R.

The Indian attacks continued. On June 24 about forty Arapahoes attacked Sweetwater Station, killing one soldier and wound-

---

[9] Pennock *loc. cit.,* 9; Walker, *loc. cit.,* 335.

[10] Pennock, *loc. cit.,* 11; Walker, *loc. cit.,* 335.

ing another.[11] On June 26, when Lieutenant William Y. Drew with twenty men had a running fight two miles east of Red Buttes with two hundred warriors, two soldiers and seven horses were wounded.[12] On July 2 a detachment of Company I pursued Indians who tried to run off stock but withdrew after a sharp little skirmish at Reshaw Creek, seven miles east of Platte Station.[13] As a result of this bold attack, Major Anderson ordered detachments of troops from Companies D, H, and K to report to the station to reinforce the garrison.[14] On the morning of July 11 the men ran across Platte Bridge and drove off a band of Indians who were trying to stampede the beef herd.[15]

Lieutenant Bretney, with some Ohio soldiers, had been stationed at Platte Bridge for over a year; and when the Kansas troops moved in, there was friction, which came to a head on July 12. According to Bretney's story as reported by him to Mr. Mokler, Captain Greer of Company I tried to take over command of Platte Station from Lieutenant Bretney, but after a big row the Kansas men had to "hunt cover."[16]

Sergeant Isaac B. Pennock, who was in Captain Greer's company, told the other side of the incident in his Diary:

July 12, 1865: A large train of emigrants passed the bridge today. Seventy-five wagons bound for Montana, Idaho and the Gold Regions . . . A very disgraceful affair occured this afternoon. A number of men of "G" Co. 11th Ohio Cav. got drunk after getting a written order of their commanding officer Lieut. Britney, contrary to the orders of Capt. Greer ranking officer at this place. Capt. Greer gave permission to emigrants to camp one mile or farther across the river from company. Lieut. Britney came to his tent and in a boisterious and insulting manner demanded to know who commanded here. The Capt. told him he did. The Lieut. told him he did not that he

---

[11] Pennock, *loc. cit.,* 10.
[12] *Ibid.,* 11.
[13] *Ibid.,* 12.
[14] Fairfield, *loc. cit.,* 356.
[15] Pennock, *loc. cit.,* 15.
[16] Mokler, *Fort Caspar,* 20.

was commander here and he was going to make those emegrants leave where they were camped. The Capt. told him that he must not interfere with them that he was ranking officer here at this place and he had given them permission to camp anywhere a mile or farther from the bridge. The Lieut. demanded to see his written authority to command him. The Capt. told him he acted from seniority and superiority of rank and told him he wished him not to interfere with the emigrants as he had authorized them to camp on the other side of the river, one mile from camp. The Lieut. left in a passion. His men went to the emegrant camp, got drunk, fired into it several shots narrowly missing two persons, one a young child. One fired from the bridge with a Spencer rifle, the ball narrowly missing some person in the train. Some drew there arms on our boys and struck one as he was on duty carrying a dispatch to the telegraph operator for transmission. Lieut. Britney ran the telegraph operator out of the office twice cocking arms and threatening to shoot him. The operator came to the Capt. tent and asked permission for a place to sleep saying he was fearful for his life if he remained over night and slept with the Capt. and myself one of the members of the night company, Kelly was run off from the station and had to remain over night with our camp in his escape from them he lost his hat coming into our camp bareheaded. Sergeant Holding of our camp being at the well of the station having a wound dressed which he received in a battle with the Indians on Sunday week ago was accosted by one of them and was told he wished to God the ball had gone through his brain—this in the hearing of Lieut. Britney. The emigrants asked protection of Capt. Greer against the Ohio troops as they were more fearful of them than the Indians. July 13, 1865 . . . Whiskey about out over at post—it was what was the matter. If Lieut. Britney had given orders for whiskey for his men there would have been no disgraceful conduct on the part of his men. He is chiefly to blame for all the trouble yesterday. His own men cocked their guns on him and threatened to shoot him and he was unable to do anything with them, or at least did not.[17]

This conflict between the Ohio and Kansas troops must have created much ill feeling, because when Major Anderson arrived on July 16 with forty men of Company K to take command of all

---

[17] Pennock, *loc. cit.,* 15–16.

troops from Fort Laramie to South Pass, he promptly ordered Lieutenant Bretney and his men to Sweetwater Station.[18]

With this background it is possible to understand Major Anderson's antagonism toward Lieutenant Bretney and his ordering Lieutenant Caspar Collins, an Ohio officer, to lead the relief party, which consisted of Kansas troops, on July 26, instead of one of his Kansas officers. On July 14 Lieutenant R. J. Harper, with the noncommissioned staff and the brass band, started for Fort Leavenworth for muster-out. They were relieved at Platte Station by fourteen men of the Third U. S. Infantry Volunteers. These were "Galvanized Yankees," or Southern soldiers who had been recruited from Rebel camps for service against the Indians.[19]

The detachment of forty men of Company K which had arrived at Platte Bridge with Major Anderson on July 16 was sent on a scout westward as far as Horse Creek. It returned to Deer Creek on July 21, but according to the company muster roll, ten men who were engaged in the action of July 26 were left at Platte Bridge. These were probably the same ten men who escorted the mail to Platte Bridge under the command of Corporal Henry Grimm the day before the action.

Back at Horseshoe Station, Company H was having Indian troubles. Captain Joel Huntoon included a description of several skirmishes in his muster roll dated August 31, 1865:

> On the 22nd [July] the Company went out on a scout and run into a squad of Indians supposed to be 30 in number capturing their horse equipments and killing two of their ponies. Distance 16 miles. 25th sent out scout got on trail of Indians pursued about 20 miles returned making 90 miles traveled.

All of the remaining companies of the Eleventh Kansas Cavalry, which were scattered along the Oregon Trail from Fort Laramie to South Pass, hourly expected orders to return to Fort

---

[18] Mokler, *Fort Caspar,* 20.
[19] Spring, *op. cit.,* 83; Walker, *loc. cit.,* 336.

Leavenworth for mustering out. Their three-year term of enlistment would expire in September. These grizzled veterans had suffered through three years of war, pestilence, and famine, and had buried their dead on many distant camps and battlefields. They were tired of this barren, desolate country and eagerly awaited the orders which would return them to their homes in the green hills of eastern Kansas.

3

The Wagon Train

During the Civil War all the available men and supplies had been diverted to the embattled armies in the East, leaving only skeleton forces with scant supplies to hold back the Indians on the western frontier. When the war ended at Appomattox in April, 1865, the badly needed rations and supplies could be sent to the distant posts, and loaded wagon trains were sent out from the depots in the East.[1]

In the middle of July a wagon train arrived at Horseshoe Station, eighty-five miles west of Fort Laramie, held by Company H, Eleventh Kansas Cavalry. It resumed its journey westward on July 17; and since it was entering country where roving bands of Indians prowled along the Oregon Trail, it was accompanied by sixteen dismounted men of Company H under the command of Commissary Sergeant Amos Jefferson Custard. With horses and mules so scarce, there was no object in mounting the escort, as it could march at the same rate as the wagons traveled—about two and one-half miles an hour, or twenty to twenty-five miles a day. At La Bonté Station eleven men of Company D, Eleventh Kansas Cavalry, under Corporal James W. Shrader, joined the escort.

The little detachment reached Platte Station, where three of

[1] Walker, *loc. cit.*, 336.

PLATTE BRIDGE STATION

From a drawing by bugler C. Moellman, Co. G, Eleventh Ohio Cavalry, in 1863.

Reprinted by permission of the publishers, The Arthur H. Clark Company, from Hebard and Brininstool, The Bozeman Trail.

Courtesy of Fort Caspar Commission

Courtesy of Fort Caspar Commission

LIEUTENANT CASPAR COLLINS LIEUTENANT HENRY C. BRETNEY

Both from paintings by Ruth Joy Hopkins

Courtesy of Victoria Shrader

JAMES W. SHRADER

LIEUTENANT WILLIAM Y. DREW

*Courtesy of Mabel Drew Thorburn
and Ethel Drew Truitt*

the men of Company H remained.[2] On Friday, July 21, the supply train and escort set out for Sweetwater Station, also called Fort Stillings, fifty-two miles to the west. They were accompanied by Lieutenant Bretney with forty men of Company G, Eleventh Ohio Cavalry, ordered to Sweetwater by Major Anderson, Sergeant Merwin remaining with three men to serve the twelve-pound mountain howitzer. The supply train now consisted of five six-mule army wagons loaded with rations and supplies and the tents and baggage of Company G.[3] The wagons were unloaded at Sweetwater Station, and on the morning of Tuesday, July 25, the empty wagons and escort started back to Platte Station, where they were scheduled to arrive at noon on July 26.

Although another man had originally been slated to command the escort when it left Horseshoe, Sergeant Custard, leader of the hard core of veterans which comprised the little detachment, had volunteered to take his place upon payment of four hundred dollars.[4] At this time he was thirty-seven years of age and, judging from his photograph, about six feet in height, of medium build, with blue eyes and black hair, mustache, and beard.

Custard had been born in Crawford County, Pennsylvania, in 1827, the eldest of seven children. His father, Robert Ward Custead, had been born in 1799, while his mother, Lydia Sitler, had been born in 1800. Lydia was the daughter of Jacob Sitler and Catherine Foust Sitler and the granddaughter of Baron Dietrich Sitler and Anna Marie Von Resler. The Custead children, then, were of English descent on their father's side and of

[2] "On the 17 day of July a detachment of 16 men started for Platte Bridge DT on arriving there 13 of the men were sent to escort train near Platte Bridge DT to Sweetwater and when on their way back at or near Platt Bridge the 26th the Indians attacked them capturing or killing all of the men—burned the train, distance 200 miles." Muster Roll of Company H, Eleventh Kansas Cavalry, August 31, 1865, over signature of Captain Joel Huntoon.

[3] Walker, *loc. cit.,* 336; Alfred J. Mokler, *Fort Caspar,* 20, 31.

[4] The sources of this incident are Nettie Geelan Noe, the daughter of Rose's sister, now deceased; Elsie Price, granddaughter of Sergeant Custard; and Nellie Haas, niece of Sergeant Custard.

German descent on their mother's. The English name of Custead was changed by common usage to "Custard."[5]

In 1853, Amos married Rose Geelan and emigrated with her
and his brother Robert from Pennsylvania to Kansas. Their
sister, Salome Custard, came out from Pennsylvania to live with
Amos and Robert, and was married in 1860 to Patrick Geelan,
the brother of Rose. The two families lived on neighboring farms
about one mile south of Big Springs, Kansas. Amos acquired his
homestead patent to the northwest quarter of Section 14, Township 12 South Range 17 East of the 6th Principal Meridian, on
June 15, 1860.[6]

Amos and Rose had two children—Thomas, born in 1856, and
Flora Anna, born in 1857. Robert Custard died in 1860; Rose
Geelan Custard was killed in 1862 when thrown from a wagon
when the horses bolted. Although the Custards were Methodists
and Presbyterians, Amos donated seven acres in the north end
of his farm to the Big Springs Catholic Church for use as a
burial ground, and his wife was buried there. The double trag-
edy was such a blow to Custard that when Lincoln issued the call
for three more regiments from Kansas, he left Tom and Anna
with his sister Salome and went to Tecumseh, where he enlisted
in August, 1862. He was promoted from corporal to sergeant
in September, 1862, and after being found worthy of trust and
confidence, was made commissary sergeant.

The Company H muster roll states that there were thirteen
men of the company sent out to Sweetwater Station. As only
twelve can be accounted for, one man may have remained there.
It is more likely that Private Moses Brown, who was killed with

[5] All the personal data on Sergeant Custard have been furnished by John T.
W. Price, great grandson of the Sergeant, who compiled it from information
given by the descendants of Custard, the Geelan family, and Nellie Haas.

[6] This information was furnished by Harley I. Spencer, who now owns the
west eighty acres of the old Custard homestead. His father purchased it from
Custard's daughter Anna for $550. Mr. Spencer secured the technical data from
his abstract of title.

24

Lieutenant Caspar Collins, returned from Sweetwater with the detachment but went ahead with Lieutenant Bretney's party to Platte Station. All of the twelve had enlisted in August, 1862, except Private James Ballau, nineteen years old at his enlistment at Fort Leavenworth on December 30, 1863. Private Jesse E. Antram, born in McClellan, Pennsylvania, was an unmarried farmer twenty-two years of age living in Kaw Township in Jefferson County. Private William Brown, from Champaign County, Illinois, was a twenty-nine-year-old farmer when he left his wife and children in Kaw Township. Private George Heil, born in Jefferson County, New York, was an unmarried farmer residing at Tecumseh. Private August Hoppe was a brickmaker who had been born in Breslau, Germany. He was single and twenty-nine years old at the time of his enlistment. Private John Horton had been born in York County, South Carolina, but resided at Delaware in Leavenworth County, a single man and a laborer, twenty-four years of age. Private William B. Long, born in Marion, Ohio, was twenty-one years old, an unmarried farmer from Monmouth Township in Shawnee County. Private Ferdinand Schafer, a resident of Tecumseh who had been born in Germany, was an unmarried farmer twenty years of age. Private Samuel Sproul, born in Grannan, Ireland, was thirty-five years old when he left his wife and several children on the farm at Tecumseh. Private William West, a native of Hadley Mills, North Carolina, was thirty-five years old, with a wife and three children, when he left his farm near Burlingame, Kansas. Private Thomas W. Young, thirty-five years of age and born in Johnson, Indiana, was a married farmer residing in Osage County.[7]

Next in command of the supply train was Corporal James W. Shrader of Company D, a farm boy who had enlisted at Oska-

[7] All personal data on men in the detachment were obtained from Muster Rolls of Companies D and H, Eleventh Kansas Cavalry (August 31, 1865); the Muster-out Rolls of said companies; "Descriptive Roll of Kansas Volunteers, 1861–1865," *Report of the Adjutant General of the State of Kansas, 1861–1865;* and 1860 and 1865 census records.

loosa, his home town, on July 23, 1863, at the age of twenty-one. He had won his corporal's stripes on the following September 16. In personal appearance he was rather tall, of medium build, with dark hair and eyes. He had been born in Indiana on July 31, 1842, but his parents, originally from Ohio, had gone from state to state to find land and opportunity. From Indiana they moved to Illinois, then to Wisconsin and Iowa, spending one year in each state. They arrived at Oskaloosa, Kansas, on June 10, 1857, and commenced farming.[8]

Among the eleven men of Company D there were only three who had enlisted when the company was first organized in 1862, while there were several who had just recently joined up. Private Thomas Powell, twenty-eight years old, enlisted in Oskaloosa, the place of his residence, on August 18, 1862. He was an unmarried farmer who had been born in Coshockton County, Ohio. Private Edwin Summers, one of the first men to enlist, was an unmarried farmer twenty-one years old who had been born in Morgan County, Missouri. Private William H. Miller was only sixteen when he enlisted at Oskaloosa on September 4, 1862. He was an unmarried farm boy who resided in Mt. Florence County, but had been born in Dauphin County, Pennsylvania. Teamster Martin Green, an unmarried farmer born in Randolph County, Indiana, enlisted at the age of twenty-two in his home town of Rising Sun (across the river from Lecompton) in Jefferson County on August 23, 1863. He was probably a teamster on one of the wagons in the supply train. Private William D. Gray, eighteen years old, was an unmarried farmer residing in Delaware, Leavenworth County, when he signed up on October 29, 1863, at Aubrey, Kansas. Private Samuel Tull enlisted March 28, 1864, at Aubrey, Kansas, when he was eighteen. Private Jacob Zinn was also eighteen at the time of his enlistment in Rising Sun on September 1, 1863. He was an unmarried farmer

[8] Information concerning Corporal Shrader has been furnished by his daughter, Miss Victoria Shrader.

who had been born in Vermillion County, Illinois. Private John R. Zinn had not even drawn any army pay, as he entered the service at Lawrence, Kansas, on January 5, 1865, at the age of nineteen. Private Henry C. Smith was also a new recruit, having enlisted in Olathe, Kansas, on December 16, 1864, at the age of twenty. Private Bryon Swain had joined the outfit in his home town of Oskaloosa on July 23, 1863, at the age of eighteen.

The men in the supply train from Companies D and H (exclusive of the unknown man who did not return from Sweetwater Station) thus numbered twenty-three. As there was a total of twenty-five men all together, there were two others who were from other companies. Jean Wilson, the correspondent at Platte Bridge for the Leavenworth *Times*, said that in the supply train were one man of Company I, Eleventh Ohio Cavalry, and one of Company I, Eleventh Kansas Cavalry.[9] The muster rolls for these two companies for this period show that from the former one, Private Rice B. Hamilton was "Killed in action July 27th 1865, near Platte Bridge, D. T. by Indians." It may be that "July 27th" was an error on the part of the company commander and should be "July 26th." There is no mention of any soldier's being killed on July 27 near Platte Bridge, and that company was not stationed anywhere near Platte Bridge on that date. Possibly, then, Rice B. Hamilton was with Custard's detachment, probably having driven one of the wagons through from the east. He had enlisted on March 11, 1864, at Urbana, Ohio

The other soldier is believed to have been Private Adam Culp, who enlisted in September, 1863, at Fort Leavenworth. This man is generally regarded as having been killed with Lieutenant Caspar Collins in the party going to the relief of the wagon train, but none of the eyewitness accounts mention Culp. It has also been assumed that Private Moses Brown was killed with Custard, whereas he was one of the four men killed with Collins. It

[9] Jean Wilson, "Indian Fights and Atrocities," Leavenworth (Kansas) *Daily Times,* August 30, 1865.

is known that there were four privates killed with Lieutenant Collins: there are detailed descriptions of the finding of the bodies of all four. By elimination, in the list of those killed in action at Platte Bridge from Companies I and K, this leaves only Adam Culp, who is probably the remaining man with the Custard detachment. The muster rolls and adjutant reports do not give any clue as to this, merely referring to all as "Killed by Indians in Action, July 26, '65, Platte Bridge, D. T."

Corporal Shrader told in later years that he was returning with twenty-five men and was in charge of one wagon and twelve men; a sergeant had charge of the second wagon and twelve men.[10] If he meant that there were twenty-six men in all, then there was in the group another man, who is now impossible to identify. It is probable that he meant that there were twenty-five men in the party, including himself. His statement also seems to suggest that there were only two wagons in the train.

George Bent said that all the wagons had their covers on and that the government wagons, evidently of the large type, were drawn by six mules each.[11] Since they had no driver's seat, the teamsters rode on the saddle mules on the left next to the wagons.

Many types of wagons had been used during the Civil War, but experience had proved that the army-pattern six-mule wagon, although too heavy for four horses or mules, was far superior to all others. The smaller army wagon, known as the two-horse or four-horse or -mule wagon, would give out over rough country. It was too heavy for two horses and a light load and yet not heavy enough to carry twenty-five hundred or three thousand pounds, a four-horse load, when the roads were bad. The larger wagon had six bows, the smaller one four, both being painted a leaden blue with red wheels and undercarriage. The

10 Report of interview with J. W. Shrader in Atchison (Kansas) *Globe,* reprinted in *Winners of the West,* Vol. III (May, 1926), 7.

11 George Bent, letter to George E. Hyde dated May 3, 1905, MS., Coe Collection, Yale University.

lighter wagon was the forerunner of the escort wagon adopted in 1884, which could be used to carry either freight or passengers. As the wagons in Sergeant Custard's train came from a long distance with heavy loads over poor roads and were each drawn by six mules, they were undoubtedly the regular army wagons, which were the real stand-by for hauling freight in the West. At least one of the wagons had a brake which was installed on all wagons manufactured after 1863. The wagon brake, instead of the lock-chain, was a valuable improvement made during the war. It saved the time and trouble of stopping at the top of every hill to lock the wheels and again at the bottom to unlock them. All the wagons had the standard detachable feedbox on the front. When the mules were fed, the feedbox was fastened along the wagon tongue, so that the mules could all be fed at once, with three mules on either side.[12]

It had been found during the Civil War that mules were eccentric creatures reluctant to obey the commands of strangers and performed more satisfactorily when driven by teamsters with whom they were thoroughly acquainted. There was an affectionate personal relationship between a teamster and his mules which made for mutual understanding and higher efficiency. The driving of three teams of mules was a highly specialized art, and teamsters were assigned to driving certain mules for as long a period as possible. For this reason it is probable that Privates Rice B. Hamilton and Adam Culp had been detached from their companies for the purpose of driving the six-mule army wagons from the East. That Hamilton was a teamster is confirmed by his company muster roll dated June 30, 1865, which indicated that he was then on detached service carrying the mail.

---

[12] Data on army wagons have been furnished by James A. Hutchins, an authority on army transportation during this period. See also Harvey Riley, *The Mule: A Treatise on the Breeding, Training, and Uses to Which He May Be Put;* Percival G. Lowe, *Five Years a Dragoon;* and *Revised U. S. Army Regulations of 1861* (1863 ed.), 302.

Mrs. Agnes Wright Spring states that there were five wagons and fourteen teams in the train.[13] She obtained this information many years ago from Captain Bretney, John C. Friend, and others who had personal knowledge of the facts.[14] George Bent says that there were six wagons, but from all the evidence available, five seems a more likely number. The fourteen teams would be one team fewer than enough for five six-mule wagons, but after the long pull from back east it was entirely possible that two mules had given out or been killed by accident. One wagon must have got along with just two teams.

The soldiers were armed with the Smith .50 breech-loading percussion carbine,[15] which, under ideal circumstances, could be fired at the rate of fourteen shots a minute, although it was only a single-shot weapon. It was one of the early guns using fixed ammunition but was fired with a percussion cap, as there was no primer in the cartridge. A latch in front of the trigger guard released a long locking spring catch on top of the barrel, causing it to break open like a shotgun. The huge musket-type hammer on the side struck a percussion cap on a nipple, since the foil or rubber cartridges had no self-contained primer. Instead, a small tissuepaper-covered hole in the base of the cartridge was expected to burn through and permit ignition. As the army had the

[13] Spring, *op. cit.,* 61.

[14] Letter of Agnes Wright Spring to the author, October 13, 1958.

[15] Technical data on ammunition and firearms have been obtained from Gluckman's *United States Muskets, Rifles, and Carbines;* and from Philip Jay Medicus and Robert Abels, well-known authorities on the subject.

Further information is contained in a letter from H. P. White Laboratory to the author dated December 23, 1959: "We have four different specimens of the .50 Smith cartridge in our reference collection. The bullets vary in weight from 331 to 376 grains, in diameter from .521″ to .535″, and in length from .860″ to .870″. All, however, have one plain, deep cannelure very close to the base, a flat base, and a pointed nose. It is virtually impossible to make an indentification of ammunition of this period based on dimensions and weights either of fired or unfired specimens, because of the wide latitudes of dimension common at the time. The bore and groove dimensions of a Smith carbine in our reference collection are respectively .505″ and .511″. Rifling consists of three lands and grooves, right twist."

Burnside and Sharps rifles in quantity, not many of the Smith carbines were used, but were kept in reserve. The manufactured ammunition was made of rubber or lead foil covered with cardboard and used a conical bullet, but cartridge catalogues had instructions on how to make these cartridges out of newspaper or brown paper, using any conical or ball slug of the right caliber.[16] Rubber and gutta-percha cartridges were used at first but were unsatisfactory because they would stick in the chamber after firing and had to be pried out, since the weapon had no ejector. Foil cartridges were found to be more satisfactory and were used extensively. While there was generally a shortage of cartridges along the western frontier at this time, Custard's men had a good supply of them, because when they had left their posts, those remaining gave them some of their own cartridges, realizing that they were going on a dangerous mission.[17]

The men were in good spirits. Upon their arrival at Platte Station, they expected to be sent back East to be mustered out and were already congratulating themselves upon their good fortune in getting to go home after three years of hard service. The wagons were empty except for some bedding and grain for the mules,[18] so the men rode in the wagons, sprawled out in the shade of the canvas covers. The mules kicked up huge clouds of dust under the hot July sun.

Custard followed the old Oregon Trail, which ran southeast from Sweetwater Station but soon veered due east. At this point the road was from fifty to one hundred feet wide, as it was the only branch. After driving over flat country for eleven miles, the party "nooned" at Horse Creek, where there was plenty of water and grass. Ten miles farther on they descended the long, winding hill to Willow Springs, one of the regular camping

[16] Letter of Robert Abels to the author dated August 6, 1958.

[17] "Military History of the Eleventh Kansas Volunteer Cavalry," *loc. cit.*, 213.

[18] George Bent, letters to George E. Hyde dated May 15 and May 22, 1906, MS., Coe Collection, Yale University.

31

places, which derived its name from the stunted trees which lined the creek. It was an outstanding spot on the Oregon Trail and, to travelers over this arid region, literally an oasis in the desert. The train probably stopped here to water the mules and then continued three miles down Willow Creek to the little meadow south of the road at Lower Willow Springs, where camp was made for the night. The wagon train was now about halfway to Platte Station and, if it got an early start in the morning, should arrive there at noon the next day.

That afternoon about two o'clock a mounted detachment of ten men of Company G, Eleventh Ohio Cavalry, commanded by Lieutenant Bretney, accompanied by Captain A. Smyth Lybe of the Sixth U. S. Infantry left Sweetwater Station for Fort Laramie by way of Platte Bridge to draw pay for their companies. Finding the wagon train encamped at Lower Willow Springs, Bretney's party halted here for two hours for supper and to rest their horses but left about nine o'clock for Platte Bridge, where they arrived at two o'clock the next morning. Bretney tried to persuade Sergeant Custard to bring the wagon train in with him, but the Sergeant thought the mules too tired.[19] Neither party had seen any Indians since leaving Sweetwater Station, and there was no reason to believe that the Indians had concentrated near Platte Station. They could not possibly have known of fighting there on July 25 because the telegraph wire was down west of there. When Bretney arrived at Platte Station, he first learned of the fighting and was surprised that his party had not been attacked.[20]

Sergeant Custard had his little party on the road early the

[19] Pennock, *loc. cit.*, 19; Spring, *op. cit.*, 82; Mokler, *Fort Caspar*, 26.

[20] Walker, *loc. cit.*, 336; William Y. Drew, "The Indian Fight at Platte Bridge Station," Osage County *Chronicle*, April 27, 1882.

The evidence is conflicting on this point. Mrs. Spring, who received her information directly from Bretney, does not say that Indians were seen or heard by him on his trip to Platte Bridge. Mr. Mokler, who received his data from a son of Bretney, says that during the trip Bretney heard cries which he knew meant war and saw Indians moving across the hills (Mokler, *Fort Caspar*, 26).

next morning. As they left their camp, the trail swerved towards the northeast, leaving the creek. There would be no more usable water until they reached the North Platte River east of the Red Buttes. After driving four miles, the wagon train crossed the alkali flats at the crossing of Poison Creek. Since the water was too bitter to drink, they hurried on four miles farther, where the road ascended a slope between two rock formations called "Rock Avenue." The long, narrow, jagged formation on the north was sometimes called the "Devil's Backbone." Two miles farther east the road divided, the north branch going up to cross the divide at Emigrant Gap, while the telegraph road sloped southeast towards the North Platte River before turning eastward up over the divide. As Custard was next seen at the river near Red Buttes, he took the south road. His men and animals had been without water since leaving camp.

About eight o'clock, after going another five miles, Sergeant Custard came to the place where the telegraph road ran close to the river bend east of Red Buttes. Here he found a telegraph patrol of thirty men of the Eleventh Ohio Cavalry with their wagons drawn up close in line across the neck of a peninsula, forming a good breastwork, with rifle pits dug along the river bank. The patrol had tried several days before to reach Platte Bridge, but were driven back by mounted warriors who completely blockaded the way and angrily motioned them back. Since the telegraph line was down for at least nine miles, it was folly to try to repair it. The Pacific Coast received no telegraphic news for seven days. This was the third day of siege, and the faint boom of the howitzer could be heard from Platte Bridge only nine miles away. The appearance of the wagon train was

As Bretney made the last part of his trip at night, from nine o'clock in the evening until two o'clock in the morning, it is difficult to believe that he saw Indians and heard their cries, because it was their uniform practice to stay in their camps at night, especially when they were trying to conceal their strength. Bretney's party apparently did not talk to the telegraph patrol at Red Buttes, as it would have been about midnight when it passed this place.

hailed by the telegraph patrol with great joy and satisfaction, and a cordial invitation was given them to halt and join forces for their mutual protection.[21]

> Sergeant Custard replied contemptuously, "No sir; we don't stop here. We are going into Platte Bridge in spite of all the redskins this side of Hell."
>
> "But the fort is surrounded, and thousands of Indians cover the plain this side of the bridge."
>
> "I don't care a damn. You Ohio fellows, decked out in buckskin and fringe think you know too much about this Injun business. We have been South, where fighting is done, and we know how to do it."
>
> "But you cannot get through, I tell you, and by halting here you may save all our lives. For God's sake, Sergeant, don't go on. Be a man, now, and join us and wait until the siege is over."
>
> "You fellows are skeered. We will go on, and if you want to be safe, go on with us. We will cut our way through, or go to Hell a-trying. Forward, Men!"[22]

One of Custard's men expostulated with him and asked him to stay one night, but Custard was bound to go on. If they could lick the Rebels, they were not afraid of a few Indians! He started off in the lead wagon, with Corporal Shrader bringing up the rear. The telegraph patrol watched them drive up the long dividing ridge. An hour later they disappeared from sight, hurrying in a cloud of dust to keep their appointment with Destiny.[23]

---

[21] Charles Whitehead, "Old Fort Casper," *Wyoming Historical Collections,* 288–92.

[22] *Ibid.,* 289.

[23] *Ibid.*

4

The Indians Declare War

THE MASSING OF THE HOSTILE TRIBES along the Oregon Trail and the Overland route, which brought the Eleventh Kansas Cavalry to the North Platte country as reinforcements, was the direct result of military expeditions sent against them in 1864.[1]

In the North the Teton Sioux, led by such chiefs as Four Horns, Black Moon, and Sitting Bull, roved from the Missouri westward to the lower Powder River and were openly hostile to the white invasion. They declared that no more emigrants should come through their country and that they would attack wagon trains, steamboats coming up the river, or any troops that entered their territory. In the spring of 1864 1,000 lodges of these Indians were encamped on the Missouri River above the mouth of Heart River. A strong force composed of 4,000 cavalry, 800 mounted infantry, 12 pieces of artillery and 3,000 teams was sent against them under command of Brigadier General Alfred Sully. This column went into the badlands of the Little Missouri to the head of Cannonball River and thence across country to the Upper Knife River, where the soldiers drove the tribes back after a running fight twelve miles west of

[1] The material for this chapter is taken from Grinnell, *The Fighting Cheyennes,* 216–21; Hyde, *Red Cloud's Folk,* 116–24; and George Bent, letters to George E. Hyde, dated May 4, 7, 11, 15, and 22, 1906, MS., Coe Collection, Yale University.

present-day Killdeer, Dunn County, North Dakota, which lasted three days in July, 1864. In this engagement, which was called the Battle of Killdeer Mountain, the Indians fought fiercely trying to prevent the soldiers from entering their home camp, which was on the main route of the white men. It was reported that 8,000 warriors engaged in the battle against General Sully, 311 of whom were killed and 700 wounded. The Sioux disappeared southward toward the Black Hills and thereafter ranged in the more restricted area bounded on the south by the North Platte, on the north by the Yellowstone, and on the west by the Big Horn Mountains. The army considered Sully's campaign a military success, but one result of it was that these tribes, in retaliation, joined the southern Indians the next spring in the all-out series of attacks on the whites in the North Platte country.[2]

Farther south Colonel Chivington, with a force of Colorado Volunteers, surprised a village of Southern Cheyennes under Black Kettle at Sand Creek in Colorado on November 29, 1864, and killed many warriors, women, and children. The Indians were incensed at this attack because they claimed that the village located at Sand Creek was at peace under an agreement with the army. Many Southern Cheyennes and Arapahoes started northward after the attack and raided all white settlements and emigrant trains. They captured and killed nine white men who had been soldiers at Sand Creek and possessed Indian scalps and trinkets taken from the field. After the capture of Julesburg, Colorado Territory, this large force crossed the South Platte River and went to the Black Hills of present-day South Dakota, where they made winter camp on Bear Lodge River.[3]

Among these Indians were George Bent and Charles Bent, sons of William Bent, the founder of Bent's Fort on the Arkansas River in Colorado. George was a son of his father's first

2 Hebard and Brininstool, *The Bozeman Trail*, I, 125.

3 George Bent, letter to George E. Hyde dated May 4, 1906, MS., Coe Collection, Yale University.

wife, a Southern Cheyenne named Owl Woman, while Charles was a son of his father's second wife, a Southern Cheyenne named Yellow Woman and sister of the first wife. George Bent was an educated Indian who had gone to school at Westport, Missouri, and lived in St. Louis from 1857 to 1861. When the Civil War broke out, he joined General Price's army at Springfield, Missouri, and fought with the Confederates at the battles of Wilson's Creek and Pea Ridge. He came west in 1862 and, after visiting his family at Bent's Fort, joined the Southern Cheyenne tribe in 1863 and spent the rest of his life with them. His preference for his mother's people might be explained by the fact that his appearance of a full-blooded Indian may have prevented his full acceptance in white society. In the Julesburg raid he captured an officer's uniform from an express car and wore it in several battles.[4] In later years he wrote a series of letters from his home at Colony, Oklahoma, to George E. Hyde, in which he described his life and adventures among the Indians, most of which are now part of the Coe collection in the Yale University Library.

The winter camp had not been long on Bear Lodge River before runners came in from the Northern Cheyennes bringing word that the latter were encamped on Powder River and that there were plenty of buffalo there. In a few days the camp moved to join their relatives on Powder River. After it was learned the Sioux had moved east and the Northern Arapahoes were encamped on Powder River west of the Northern Cheyennes, runners were sent to all these camps to tell them about the massacre of the friendly Indians at Sand Creek.[5]

In early March the Southern Cheyennes and Arapahoes reached the big village on Powder River, where they found the Northern Cheyennes camped with the Oglala Sioux under Old Man Afraid of his Horses and Red Cloud. After much visiting

[4] *Ibid.*, May 7, 1906.
[5] *Ibid.*, May 4, 1906.

and feasting, they all moved down the river where wood and grass were more plentiful. The three tribes were together in one long camp extending at least three miles along the river. After three weeks here with scalp dances every night, scouts were sent out to find buffalo, as game was getting scarce. Since it had driven away the game, drumming was not allowed any more. The scouts found a buffalo herd toward the south on Little Powder River, and the village arrived here after two moves. It was now April, but the grass would not be good until the middle of May. Although the horses were not in shape to go out yet, the tribes began to plan for a big war party against the soldiers. During the councils the Southern Cheyennes told about the outrages committed by the soldiers at Sand Creek and displayed many horses and plunder which they had captured during the raids while coming north. The Northern Sioux told about their fight with General Sully and, because they had lost territory and had sustained heavy losses in battle, were eager to join with the other tribes in the war. The few chiefs who were still friendly to the government were overruled, and the Powder River tribes accepted the war pipe offered them by the Southern Cheyennes. Thus war was declared on the white man.[6]

In May the big village moved westward to Tongue River and followed the buffalo up the river. The Northern Cheyennes all camped together in a horseshoe circle, in the center of which were the two medicine lodges, the Medicine Arrow Lodge on the right and the Buffalo Hat Lodge on the left. The opening of the village faced the west, the direction in which the camp was moving. The Red Cloud Sioux camped to the rear of the Cheyennes, one-half mile back, not in a circle but with the six soldier bands, or societies, and the band of chiefs extended in a long line. The six societies were the Crooked Lances or Bone Scrapers, the Bow Strings, the Foolish (Crazy) Dogs, the Dog Soldiers, the Foxes, and the Red Shields. George Bent, Roman Nose, and

6 *Ibid.*, May 7, 1906; Hyde, *op. cit.*, 116–17.

CORPORAL AMOS JEFFERSON CUSTARD

Courtesy of Elsie Price

THOMAS AND FLORA ANNA CUSTARD

Courtesy of Elsie Price

COLONEL PRESTON B. PLUMB

MAJOR MARTIN ANDERSON

CAPTAIN JOEL HUNTOON

LIEUTENANT GEO. M. WALKER

All photographs courtesy of Kansas State Historical Society

Young Man Afraid of His Horses all belonged to the Crooked Lances. The chiefs of all the tribes were holding councils of war and notified the societies that war parties would start out as soon as the horses got fat but would not make any raids until June. In the meantime the chiefs would consider the best places to make the raids. After camping at the foot of the Big Horn Mountains, they moved over to Powder River again, following the buffalo. It took a lot of meat for such a large village.[7]

In June several large war parties left the village. The band of Cheyennes which George Bent accompanied struck the North Platte River fifty miles below Platte Bridge, where it drove away a herd of mules after fighting with the soldiers, who took refuge in the stockade. This could have been the fight at La Prelle Station, where Captain Marshall of Company E of the Eleventh Ohio Cavalry lost his stock. The next day this war party went up to Platte Bridge and, as the river was high, fought with the soldiers across the river with guns, but no one was hurt. That evening, when a large mule train was reported coming up the south side of the river, the Indians swam their horses across the river and charged on the mules when they were being led to water. The herders fled to the train, and the soldiers fired from long range. The white bell mare ran up the river (westward) followed by the 250 mules, most of which had the US brand on them. One of the Indians caught the bell mare and led her across the river to the north side, all the other mules following her. The war party returned with the herd of mules to the village found on Lodgepole Creek. Another war party of Cheyennes had returned with much plunder, while a band of Red Cloud Sioux had captured many horses and mules east of Fort Laramie. There was much feasting and dancing in celebration of these victories.[8]

After all the war parties had returned, the chiefs held a war council. There must have been one thousand lodges in the village

[7] George Bent, letter to George E. Hyde dated May 11, 1906, MS., Coe Collection, Yale University.

[8] *Ibid.*

composed of Oglalas, Miniconjous, Brûlés, Sans Arcs, and Northern and Southern Cheyennes and Arapahoes. It was decided that no more small war parties would leave and that no one could run buffalo by himself, but that a big raid would be made at Platte Bridge from Crazy Woman Creek. Platte Bridge was selected because it was the last crossing of the North Platte, and its capture would disrupt emigrant movements and cut the soldiers' line in two. The time had not been set to start, but all the warriors were told to prepare for it. The Foolish Dog Soldiers were selected to act as police and were instructed that if anyone should steal away from the village, he would be whipped and his horses killed. When the news was brought to the societies by the criers, war dances commenced and everyone started to get ready for the big raid. All the charms that were worn in battle were fixed up. New feathers were put on war bonnets, shields, and lances; and scalps were sewed into the scalp shirts, for it was believed that any warrior who went into battle without their having been repaired would be killed or wounded. All this was done by the medicine men, who invoked the blessings of the Great Spirit while being feasted by the warriors.[9]

The village moved to Crazy Woman Creek. After camping there several days, the chiefs announced that the warriors would march for Platte Bridge the next day. The soldier bands were ordered to paint their war horses for battle and to put on all their war bonnets, shields, lances, scalp shirts, and medicine charms. Those who got ready first rode out half a mile beyond the opening of the circle of the village and waited until everybody else got there. Each band formed in line, the first ones in battle taking the lead, followed by two men in each line with four men in the rear. The bands rode around inside the circle of the village with the Foolish Dogs in front and the Dog Soldiers in the rear. As the Sioux and Arapahoes took part also, the line was about two miles long. Everybody was singing war songs, the

9 *Ibid.*, May 15, 1906.

women and old men standing in front of their lodges singing as the bands rode by at a trot. That night there was singing and dancing all through the village. The horses were kept in the center of the village so they could be caught up easily.[10]

The war party set out the next morning, but did not go very far the first day so that everybody could come up. The Cheyennes were led by Dull Knife, White Bull, and Roman Nose, while Red Cloud, Old Man Afraid of His Horses, and Young Man Afraid of His Horses were the Sioux chiefs. All the bands camped together, while the chiefs of the three tribes were always ahead to locate the camp for the night. The Foolish Dogs, who acted as police in the march, took the lead and also brought up the rear to see that everybody kept in line. The chiefs rode ahead and, upon discovering water, would stop so that everybody could water his horses and smoke his pipe while resting.[11]

Before arriving at Platte Bridge, the chiefs selected several warriors to go ahead and find out how many soldiers were there. These returned the same evening, and the war party stopped to camp on a small stream with no timber on it. George Bent estimated that there were three thousand Indians in the party. Criers were sent out that night to announce that no singing would be allowed. The next morning, July 25, the chiefs selected ten warriors to follow down the creek, which came out a short distance below Platte Bridge, to try to draw the soldiers toward the big hill behind which the Indians planned to conceal themselves. If they could get the soldiers this far out from the bridge, they could kill them all before they could get back. The Foolish Dog Soldiers got on both sides of the whole line of the war party, and the Dog Soldiers got in the rear and bunched up the line from the rear. There was a long column, with the chiefs in the lead. Red Cloud and Old Man Afraid of His Horses had their scalp shirts on. Everybody was told not to go faster than a walk so that

10 *Ibid.*
11 *Ibid.*

41

dust would not be thrown up and the soldiers apprised that a large party was coming. The chiefs stopped behind the big hill five or six miles north of the bridge and crawled to the top with spyglasses to see if the scouts had reached the mouth of the creek. Now all the medicine making commenced. All were notified to get ready for the fight. War bonnets were taken out of the sacks, while the medicine bonnets were held by the owners to the south first, then to the west, then to the north, then to the east, and last to the sun, before they were put on. Medicine shields were held in the right hand and dipped four times on the ground, then held up to the sun and shaken four times, then placed in the left hand, as the right hand was used to carry lances, war clubs, or rifles.[12]

As the chiefs looked down into the valley, Dull Knife, the Northern Cheyenne chief, said in a loud voice that soldiers were crossing the bridge. Firing was heard and all rushed and looked over the hill. The soldiers were firing the cannon at the scouts but would not follow them, so the scouts returned about noon. They reported that the river was very high and that they swam their horses over the river below the bridge. While attempting to run off some stock, they had had a fight with soldiers on the south side of the river, where the Cheyenne chief, High Wolf, had been killed. The little stream which the scouts followed down was known as "Dry Creek" but is now called "Casper Creek" and runs southeasterly into the North Platte River about half a mile northeast of Platte Bridge.

That night the Indians camped behind the big hill two miles north of the bridge. All remained concealed except the scouts so that the garrison would not know about the large war party. Since there were too many soldiers in the stockade to risk a direct attack, it was determined that a small decoy party would try to draw them out of the fort and then all the hidden warriors

12 *Ibid.,* May 22, 1906.

42

would try to cut them off. After that it would be an easy matter to take over the stockade.[13]

Before daylight a party of Sioux were sent down the little creek to conceal themselves in the willows and cottonwoods on both sides of the river east of the little post. George Bent stayed with the larger party behind the big hill. The Dog Soldiers went west of the bridge next to the river, behind some small bluffs. The telegraph road ran between the hill on the north and the river, so that a trap was formed along the road on both sides of the stockade. Soldiers coming out would be cut off, no matter which direction they might take. The massed Indian tribes had not been discovered, as Jules Seminoe, the Frenchman who was married to a Shoshoni woman and who was at the time working for the government at the stockade, later told George Bent that the soldiers had no idea that the large war party was there.[14] They thought it was just a small party to run off the stock. While many estimates placed the number of warriors from 2,500 to 3,000, the report of General P. E. Connor of July 27, 1865, that 1,000 Indians had attacked Platte Station, seems more realistic.[15]

By daylight all the warriors were concealed in their positions, ready to spring the trap whenever the soldiers were enticed from the fort.

[13] *Ibid.*
[14] *Ibid.*
[15] U. S. Serial Set [U. S. Congress], Serial 3436, *H.R. Doc. 369,* Pt. 1, p. 357.

5

Prelude at Platte Station

WHILE THE WARRIORS of the combined tribes were marching on Platte Station, small unattached bands continued to harass the Oregon Trail posts. After Captain Greer had his skirmish with the Indians at Reshaw Creek, seven miles east of the bridge, July 2, Major Anderson took steps to reinforce his little garrison. Sergeant Custard's detachment from Companies D and H had reported and been sent to Sweetwater Station on escort duty, leaving three men of Company H. Corporal Grimm with some men from Company K, who were to bring the mail from Deer Creek was expected daily. The main force at the post was seventy men of Company I, Eleventh Kansas Cavalry, under Captain Greer, Lieutenant Clancy, and Lieutenant Drew. Because the weather was very hot, the company was camped in tents along the riverbank east of the post. Lieutenant George M. Walker of the Eleventh Kansas Cavalry was acting post adjutant. There were also the fourteen galvanized troops of the Third U. S. Infantry, which had replaced the noncommissioned staff who had gone back east to be mustered out. Sergeant Merwin and three men of Company G, Eleventh Ohio Cavalry were in charge of the twelve-pound mountain howitzer.[1] Two tipis of Shoshoni

1 Mokler, *Fort Caspar,* 13, 31.

Indians, employed as scouts for the government, were encamped outside the stockade.[2]

During the recent hostilities the feelings of savage hate against the Indians had become intensified. Private Bonwell had been tortured and mutilated. In the fight at Sweetwater Station on June 24, a soldier had been horribly tortured and dismembered. All of his hair had been scalped, his hands cut off at the wrists, the sinews taken out of his arms, his heart and liver cut out, a lance run into him, and his body stuck up on a pole. The boys swore that if ever they got hold of an Indian, they would cut him all to pieces.[3] Tension mounted with each attack.

On Saturday night, July 22, five horses were stolen by a party of ten Indians and one white man, and the next morning Captain Greer with twenty-six men pursued but were unable to overtake them. The telegraph wires were cut on both sides of the station, and Lieutenant Walker was sent out with a party to repair the line to the east so that communication would be restored with Deer Creek Station. He was attacked by an overwhelming force of Indians and compelled to retreat to the post with the loss of one man killed and several wounded. Private Baker of Company K was thrust through the body with a bayonet used as a lance, the bayonet remaining in the wound. A comrade pulled it out with great effort, and Baker survived.[4] William R. Glover of Company I was wounded in the wrist and side.[5] That night Indians were around the post. Sentinel Stenkbery saw two of them; but since the night was dark, he did not get a shot at them. Just before daybreak Corporal May fired on them but did not hit

[2] *Ibid.,* 16.

[3] Pennock, *loc. cit.,* 10; Mokler, *Fort Caspar,* 18, 19; Drew, *loc. cit.,* April 20, 1882.

[4] "Military History of the Eleventh Kansas Volunteer Cavalry," *loc. cit.,* 211.

[5] "Roster of the Eleventh Kansas Cavalry Regiment," *Report of the Adjutant General of the State of Kansas, 1861–1865.*

anyone.[6] The mail was delayed at Horseshoe Station on account of Indians in that vicinity.[7]

On Monday night, July 24, at the time when the big war party arrived at the hill six miles to the northeast, there was considerable restlessness among the horses at the post. The men knew that Indians were prowling nearby, as the delicate nostrils of the horses could detect them from a great distance.[8]

Although the morning of the next day was uneventful, in the afternoon the soldiers got a preview of things to come. Lieutenant William Y. Drew of Company I, Eleventh Kansas Cavalry, observed part of the action:

> Just after dinner on the 25th of July, 1865, someone called out "Indians," and all hands, seizing their arms, ran out to see where they were, their number, and so forth. On the north side of the river about 15 or 20 Indians on horseback were moving leisurely along. In a few minutes about a dozen men mounted, and crossing the bridge, they skirmished with the enemy. As fast as our men moved on, the Indians fell back, until our men had gone about three miles from the bridge. All this time the Indians were increasing in numbers, until there were about forty in plain sight. Our boys had been using their carbines with good effect, and had shot several Indians off their ponies without any particular loss or damage to our side. At this time an order was received from the station for the men to come back, as the Indians were showing themselves on the south side of the river, east of the station. As our men fell back toward the bridge, Indians kept coming out of the ravine, until there were about fifty in sight, showing that their maneuvering had been for the purpose of leading our men as far away from all support as possible, and to then wipe them out by superior numbers. Our men reached the station without any loss.[9]

This little skirmish probably lasted from one o'clock until about three o'clock. The horse herd, which had been grazing

---

[6] Pennock, *loc. cit.*, 18.

[7] *Ibid.*

[8] *Ibid.*

[9] Drew, *loc. cit.*, April 20, 1882.

on the south side of the river below the tents of Company I, was driven into the stockade. As the soldiers returned, the Indians followed them and hovered about the post. The long-awaited mail ambulance from Deer Creek Station arrived at Platte Bridge about four o'clock, escorted by ten men of Company K, who had been ordered to Platte Bridge as reinforcements, under the command of Corporal Grimm. Lieutenant Caspar W. Collins of the Eleventh Ohio Cavalry rode in the ambulance with the mail.[10]

Lieutenant Collins had been second in command of Company G under Lieutenant Bretney, ever since the death of Captain L. M. Rinehart and was promoted to the rank of first lieutenant on May 1, 1865, although he was never mustered to that office.[11] He had gone to Fort Laramie with an escort of ten men to obtain more horses for the company. After the horses were sent on, Collins remained there a few days until he was ordered by General Connor to join his company. He left Fort Laramie about July 21, althought it was known that the Indians were watching all roads.

Caspar W. Collins had been born at Hillsboro, Ohio, on September 30, 1844, the son of William Oliver Collins, who later became colonel of the Eleventh Ohio Cavalry. In 1862, Colonel Collins, ordered west to guard the emigrant roads, brought his son Caspar with him. Upon returning to Ohio, the boy was commissioned a second lieutenant on June 30, 1863, and was sent back west, having been assigned to Company G of the Eleventh Ohio Cavalry. Lieutenant Collins was well liked and became quite friendly with the Indians around Fort Laramie. In personal appearance he was described as a mere boy, slight and delicate, but was reputed to be a good rider and a fine hunter, speaking the Sioux language fluently.[12]

[10] Walker, *loc. cit.*, 336.

[11] Spring, *op. cit.*, 82.

[12] All data on Lieutenant Caspar Collins are taken from Spring, *Caspar Collins.*

The driver of the mail ambulance reported that Indians were endeavoring to stampede the beef herd, which was grazing in a valley about two miles east of the station. Captain Greer, with sixteen men of Company I, accompanied by Corporal Grimm's squad—about thirty men in all—went to the relief of the herders.[13] The Indians, who had swum their ponies across the river, fell back before the charges of the soldiers but gradually increased their numbers. In one of the charges a Cheyenne chief was shot through the bowels and threw his arm over the neck of his pony, which wheeled to the left and went into a thicket of brush, where the chief fell off. The Indians charged desperately to drive back the men so as to rescue their fallen chief, but a reinforcement of about a dozen men came up from the station, and the Indians were repulsed. They were finally driven across the river about dark, when a number of them appeared across the river from the post, making all sorts of ludicrous demonstrations, but a few shots caused them to diperse.[14] A steer which the Indians had killed was stuck and hauled into camp.[15]

As the command returned, Privates Henry Lord and Jim Porter of Company I were sent to investigate and found the chief, High Wolf, the leader of the decoy party, lying apparently dead. They jumped off their horses and stabbed the Indian about the heart. He did not give the least sign of life. Then the troopers commenced to scalp him. As soon as the knife touched his head, the Indian began to beg them not to scalp him, but one of the men shot him through the brain. The Indians believed that if a warrior lost his scalp, he could not go to the happy hunting grounds. They would lose their lives without the least sign of fear, but wanted to save their scalps. The boys took the chief's arms and buckskin jacket, which was trimmed with about thirty-five different kinds of hair which he had taken at different times

13 Walker, *loc. cit.,* 336.
14 Waring, *loc. cit.,* August 26, 1909.
15 Pennock, *loc. cit.,* 18.

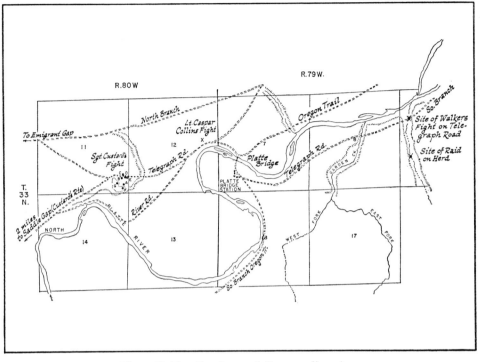

Platte Bridge Station and Surrounding Area

during his career, including hair of men, women, and children—both white and Indian. The body of High Wolf was removed that night by his father, Blind Wolf. The next morning Lord and Porter tied the chief's scalp to a stick and went down by the riverside to flaunt the trophy at some young braves riding about on the other side.[16]

From all the accounts and as indicated on Lieutenant Walker's map, this skirmish took place two miles east of the post in the valley of a little stream running northward into the river. The beef herd had been kept here, while the horse herd was closer to the post but east of the tents of the Company I men. The site of the action is now in the city of Casper, in the vicinity of Tenth Avenue and Cedar Street. It would be useless to attempt to find relics of the engagement here.

Although the men were not disturbed during the night, Major Anderson ordered them to strike their tents and retreat into the post. The fight had resulted in the killing and wounding of several Indians, but all the soldiers reported for duty on return to the stockade that evening. "No loss to our men. One was struck several times with a saber in the hands of a brave warrior, and another grazed on the hand by a ball."[17]

Everyone felt elated over the action, but on inspection of arms and ammunition that evening it was found that there were fewer than twenty rounds per man for the Smith carbines and very little more for the other arms. No cartridges for the Smith carbines had been sent to the Eleventh Kansas Cavalry since their departure from Fort Riley the preceding winter. Requisition had been made to the ordnance officials at Fort Laramie without success. Ironically, at this time Sergeant H. Todd and Corporal W. H. Smith, with an escort, were on their way from

16 "Henry Lord of Dodge City Tells of the Battle of Platte Bridge," *Indian Depredations and Battles,* clippings, Vol. III, 173–75; from Emporia (Kansas) *Gazette,* August 9, 1934.

17 Wilson, *loc. cit.,* August 30, 1865.

Fort Laramie with ordnance supplies, but that did not help the men in the present crisis.[18]

The scarcity of ammunition and supplies was due to the heavy rains along the road which prevented supply trains from getting through. This condition was described in a report of Major General Dodge, in command at Fort Leavenworth, to his superior, Major General John Pope:

> MAJOR GENERAL JOHN POPE,   FORT LEAVENWORTH
>   SAINT LOUIS: July 29, 1865
> ... General Connor [at Fort Laramie] is laboring under great difficulty. His troops are mutinous—demand their discharge. Stores that should have been at Laramie six weeks ago are stuck in the mud, and the columns here started out half-shod and half-rationed. ... Every regiment that has come here so far has been dismounted or horses unserviceable. I have not horses enough to mount even an escort, but we will overcome it all if it will only stop raining and let us have a few weeks solid road.[19]

Some of the men commenced running bullets and making Smith cartridges, Private James E. Bush being one who was very proficient in this work.[20] The Spencer cartridges, used by the Eleventh Ohio troops, could not be reloaded, while the galvanized infantry used the old Springfield muskets.[21]

At two o'clock in the morning horses were heard clattering over the bridge. When the newcomers were challenged by the sentry, the garrison was agreeably surprised to find Lieutenant Bretney with an escort of ten men of Company G of the Eleventh Ohio Cavalry and Captain Lybe of the Sixth U. S. Infantry arriving from Sweetwater Station.[22] Although these detachments were just passing through on their way to Fort Laramie to draw

---

[18] "Military History of the Eleventh Kansas Volunteer Cavalry," *loc. cit.*, 212; Drew, *loc. cit.*, April 27, 1882.

[19] *The War of the Rebellion,* Series II, Vol. 48, p. 1132.

[20] Drew, *loc. cit.*, April 27, 1882.

[21] *Ibid.*, April 20, 1882.

[22] Spring, *op. cit.*, 85.

51

pay for their companies, they would be of help during the present crisis.

> Upon his arrival at Platte Bridge the captain [Lieutenant Bretney] went at once to the quarters of Major Anderson, the commanding officer, and roused him from sleep.
>
> "Major," said Captain Bretney, "a rescue party should be sent at once to your wagon train at Willow Springs Creek to bring it here in safety. The men with their teams and wagons which you sent to Sweetwater Bridge are on their way back and are camped about twenty-five miles from here. They had gone into camp when we overtook them last night. I did my best to persuade the sergeant in command of the train to come on with us, but he said his horses were too fatigued."
>
> "They are well armed," the Major suggested.
>
> "I know that, but there is danger of the Indians surrounding them and cutting them off from all help—there are hundreds of Indians in the hills around here," Captain Bretney persisted. "We camped with the train for supper and rested our horses, leaving about 9 o'clock. Help should be sent at once—there is no time to lose," he urged. Then he left Major Anderson and went back to assist his men in getting settled for the remainder of the night.
>
> Captain Bretney was worried, and he was so sure that the Indians would make an attack on the wagon train and possibly on Platte Bridge Station that he put his horses in the square of the courtyard, enclosed by the quarters, so they could be ready for action at a moment's notice.
>
> Major Anderson evidently felt that the Captain was unduly excited as he did not send out a relief party, but retired to finish his sleep.[23]

This account, which was given by the son of Captain Bretney to Alfred James Mokler, is at variance with the evidence given by the Kansas officers, who stated that neither Custard nor Bretney had seen any signs of Indians on the trip and that the latter was surprised when he heard that the Platte Station

---

[23] Mokler, *Fort Caspar, 26–27* (used with the permission of Verne W. Mokler and Edness Mokler).

was under attack. Lieutenant Bretney apparently did not talk to the telegraph patrol near Red Buttes as he passed there about midnight. The reinforcements did not go into camp outside the stockade but put their horses into the corral and spread their blankets in the courtyard, as another attack was expected at daybreak.[24]

The personnel of the little garrison was composed of the four men of Company G, Eleventh Ohio Cavalry, who served the howitzer; the three men of Company H left behind by Sergeant Custard; the fourteen men of Company K, Third U. S. Infantry;[25] and the seventy men of Company I, Eleventh Kansas Cavalry.[26] These enlisted men, together with the five commissioned officers—Major Martin Anderson, Captain James E. Greer, Lieutenant Clancy, Lieutenant William Y. Drew, and Lieutenant George M. Walker—made a total of ninety-six men.

The arrival of the detachments of Corporal Grimm and Lieutenant Bretney at the last minute was very fortunate indeed. There were ten men of Company K, Eleventh Kansas Cavalry, under Corporal Grimm;[27] ten men of Company G, Eleventh Ohio Cavalry, under Lieutenant Bretney;[28] and the three commissioned officers—Captain Lybe, Lieutenant Bretney, and Lieutenant Caspar W. Collins—a total reinforcement of twenty-three men. This raised the strength of the garrison to 119 officers and men. If Moses Brown of Company H had come into the post with Lieutenant Bretney, the total would have been 120, although he may have been one of the three men left when Sergeant Custard first arrived there. Seventy or eighty of the men

24 Spring, *op. cit.*, 83.

25 Wilson, *loc. cit.*, August 30, 1865.

26 "Military History of the Eleventh Kansas Volunteer Cavalry," *loc. cit.*, 212.

27 The muster roll of Company K stating that ten men who were in the fight of July 26 were left behind at Platte Bridge is believed to be more accurate than the statement of Lieutenant Walker that there were twelve men in this detachment. Walker, *loc. cit.*, 336.

28 Spring, *op. cit.*, 81.

in the garrison had rifles, while half of the remainder had revolvers, the other half having no arms whatever.[29]

Since the strength of the enemy was not known, strong guards were put out, and the night was spent in preparation for whatever might occur the next day. Although only fifty to one hundred Indians had been seen, it was believed that they were only the advance of a larger war party. The men and horses were uneasy and restless: tension had increased to a high pitch, and an air of anxiety and foreboding pervaded the little garrison.[30]

[29] "Military History of the Eleventh Kansas Volunteer Cavalry," *loc. cit.*, 212.
[30] Spring, *op. cit.*, 81.

6

Lieutenant Caspar Collins' Fight

DAYBREAK ON WEDNESDAY, July 26, found Sergeant Custard pushing his little wagon train eastward along the telegraph road towards Platte Station. The war party had advanced during the night to the hills two miles north of the post, with the Dog Soldiers hidden behind the low bluffs to the west and a large party of Sioux in ambush east of the fort on both sides of the river. The trap was set. While the soldiers believed there were more Indians hiding around the post than had appeared, they had no idea of the large size of the war party.[1]

As soon as it was light, the soldiers scanned the surrounding country and saw about ninety Indians riding aimlessly around, scattered about in the hills north of the river. After breakfast the officers held a conference and decided that a party should be sent to relieve and bring in the wagon train, since it was apparent that the Indians would attack as soon as it came into sight. The question was who should lead the detachment. It was the duty of Major Anderson to stay and protect the post. Captain Greer had led the troops in the little skirmish the previous afternoon. Captain Lybe, with his infantry troops using the old Springfield muskets, was obviously unfitted for the task.

[1] George Bent, letter to George E. Hyde dated May 22, 1906, MS., Coe Collection, Yale University.

Lieutenants Walker, Drew, and Clancy were either on sick call or had other reasons for not going, so at seven o'clock Major Anderson ordered Lieutenant Collins, with Sergeant Hankhammer and Corporal Grimm, to take twenty-five men of Companies I and K and relieve the train. While Lieutenant Collins had been on the plains for three years and had had the most experience in Indian fighting, he was probably chosen because he belonged to the rival company which had caused so much trouble at the post. The Kansas officers were thus favored, as they expected momentarily to be ordered back east to be mustered out. The strongest force at the post was the ten mounted men of Lieutenant Collins' company, who were armed with the seven-shot repeating Spencer carbines that had proved so effective during the Civil War. It was needed to protect the stockade. Captain Greer had ordered Sergeant Isaac B. Pennock to take charge of the party; but when he learned that Lieutenant Collins was going to lead it, he requested that Pennock go along. Corporal Grimm reported with his ten men of Company K, who had been engaged with him in the skirmish the day before, while the balance of the party were men of Company I led by Sergeants Hankhammer and Pennock. While the latter estimated the strength of the party at twenty to twenty-five men, Mokler claimed that there were only twenty in the detachment.[2] As all of the enlisted men were Kansas troops, they were armed with the single-shot breech-loading .50 caliber Smith carbines. Lieutenant Collins was instructed not to follow the road which led west along the river bottom, but to go straight north to the top of the bluff and then turn west, keeping close to the brow of the hill which ran parallel with the road, and, upon reaching the road where it ascended to the main ridge, to follow it until he met the wagon train.[3] This way he would remain in full sight of the fort and still have a full view towards the north.

[2] Pennock, *loc. cit.,* 19; Mokler, *Fort Caspar,* 27, 29.

[3] Walker, *loc. cit.,* 337.

When he went to his fellow officer and close comrade, Captain Bretney, and asked to borrow his pistols, the captain did everything possible to dissuade him from going.

"You must not go, Caspar," the captain said. "The hills are alive with Indians—the relief should have been sent out during the night —I warned Major Anderson—it means certain death now to anyone who goes out there. I told Major Anderson at 2 o'clock this morning, and he could have sent men under the cover of darkness."

"No, Caspar," said John Friend, the telegraph operator of Sweetwater Station, who thought a great deal of the boy Lieutenant, "it is not your place to go. You don't know these men of the Eleventh Kansas—you have never soldiered with them—it's up to their officers to go—"

"I'm not a coward, John," Caspar replied.

"It's not that, it isn't always brave for a man to attempt something that is plain foolhardy. Go back and tell Anderson you won't go," Friend begged.

"I know what it means to go out there with such a small number of men, but I've never disobeyed an order," Caspar answered. "I am a soldier's son. I must go and try to rescue those men."

"I do not disobey orders, either," interrupted Captain Bretney, "but an unwise order like this one should be disobeyed; the major has no right to send you, and I told him so. He has his own officers right here, and nothing is the matter with them, they are all well and on duty—you saw they would not go if they could get out of it. They are holding back, taking no unnecessary chances, because, as they have said, they are going to be mustered out and return home in a few days."

Collins replied: "They are orders, and while I do not like them and think you are right, I have to obey them, and I am going, so lend me your pistols."

Bretney did so, and they shook hands as Bretney said: "All right; good luck, and if you find you have to come back, I will be on the other side of the river with some of our men waiting for you."

Captain Bretney at once went to Major Anderson and protested against Lieutenant Collins being sent out on this mission, first on the grounds that the number of men assigned for the hazardous undertaking was far too inadequate; second, that the men were total strangers to Lieutenant Collins, and he to them; third, that it was not in the province of Major Anderson to select this duty for Lieutenant Collins when he was under orders from General Connor, the commander of the post at Fort Laramie, to return to his own company and station, located at Sweetwater Bridge, and particularly when Major Anderson had some of his own line officers present and able to lead their own men. A captain and three lieutenants of the Eleventh Kansas Cavalry were available, and if anyone must be sent out to lead those men against this vast horde of Indians, it should be an officer whom the men knew. All this brought out some very heated argument, for Captain Bretney expressed himself in very strong language.[4]

While the dispute was taking place between Bretney and Anderson, Caspar Collins was getting ready to go on the mission. Since he did not have his horse with him, he received a powerful, high-strung, iron-gray horse which had been used by Sergeant Major Isbel. As he did not expect to return alive, he gave his cap to Private James B. Williamson of his company, telling him to keep it to remember him by. Dressing up in his new full-dress uniform which he had purchased at Fort Laramie and with a pistol in each boot top, he mounted his horse and assumed command of the little detachment.[5]

About seven-thirty o'clock the detail moved out in fine spirits, with Lieutenant Collins, jaunty and debonair, in the lead.[6] As he left, Lieutenant Walker saw two squads of Indians west of the river but south of the road, and Major Anderson ordered twenty more men to saddle up.[7] After crossing the bridge, Collins' party rode leisurely across the bottomland up onto the bluff and turned west. Lieutenant Bretney, after borrowing a Spencer carbine from Sergeant Merwin, followed along behind Collins with his ten troopers and went up on the bluff to see what

---

[4] Mokler, *Fort Caspar,* 27–28 (used with the permission of Verne W. Mokler and Edness Mokler).

[5] *Ibid.,* 30; Spring, *op. cit.,* 85.

[6] Mokler, *Fort Caspar,* 33–34.

[7] Walker, *loc. cit.,* 336–337.

action the Indians would take.[8] The infantry troops under Captain Lybe soon came up and formed a skirmish line west of Bretney along the top of the bluff to prevent the Indians from cutting off retreat to the bridge.[9] The men had been given strict orders to do no unnecessary firing on account of the shortage of ammunition. When about half a mile from the post, Collins' party turned northwest away from the edge of the bluffs and disappeared from the view of soldiers at the station.

Seeing the soldiers turn away from them, the Cheyenne Dog Soldiers hiding in the brush west of the station could restrain themselves no longer, and charged Collins' party from the south. At the same time, the Indians charged from behind the large hill to the north and out of the ravines. The Indians were all well mounted, and many had fine horses which had been stolen from emigrant trains. Because of the nature of the ground, Collins could not see the Indians approaching from the other directions, and he wheeled his men by fours left into line facing the Cheyennes coming up from the river. When he saw that he was about to be surrounded, he ordered the retreat by the left, which faced his command towards the post, leaving himself in the rear. The Cheyennes charged in three lines, while the Sioux came in squadrons. The soldiers rode pell-mell into the mass of warriors.[10]

> The Indians, coming from every side, were exposed to their own fire, and so forebore the use of bow or fire-arm, and relied mainly on spears, tomahawks and sabers. After the first discharge of carbines, which was with deadly effect, the soldiers relied wholly upon their revolvers, as there was neither time nor opportunity for reloading. The party had faced towards the station when the impossibility of proceeding further became apparent. The Indians, anxious for their prey, and confident in overwhelming numbers, rushed towards the common center in such a manner as to partially impede

[8] Mokler, *Fort Caspar,* 31.
[9] *Ibid.,* 30–31.
[10] Spring, *op. cit.,* 86.

their bloody purpose. So intermingled did the combatants become that it was impossible for the garrison to distinguish friend from foe.[11]

Back the soldiers rode, straining forward in the mad effort to reach safety. Suddenly a horse stumbled and fell, shot through the body. The soldier, prostrate, called out, "Help me! Help me! Don't leave me!" Although Collins had been shot in the hip, this was more than he could bear, so he wheeled his horse and dashed for the fallen man. After an arrow had struck him in the forehead, he maintained his seat on the horse for a short distance; then a mass of warriors surrounded him, and he disappeared in the haze of dust and smoke.[12] According to Private Waring, "They ran him to the top of the bluff and killed him. He rolled part way down the bluff which brought him in range of our guns and they left him."[13] Private S. H. Fairfield of Company K described the stampede to the bridge:

> It was a race of life. Nehring, a private of Company K, 11th Kansas, not understanding the order, dismounted to fight from a deep washout in the road. Grimm, looking around, yelled to him in German "to the bridge." That was the last that was seen of poor Nehring. Camp, also of Company K, 11th Kansas, lost his horse and then ran for dear life, but when within a few rods of safety was overtaken and tomahawked. Sergeant Hankhammer's horse was wounded, but carried him safely to the bridge and then dropped. It was a miracle that any man escaped. Our friendly Snake Indians reported that they had heard the order given by the chiefs of the wild Indians, "stop firing. You are killing our own men." This, added to the fact that the Indians were so massed, was what probably saved our boys.[14]

When Private George Camp was tomahawked five hundred yards from the river, Private W. K. Lord of Company I, lying

[11] "Military History of the Eleventh Kansas Volunteer Cavalry," *loc. cit.*, 212.

[12] George Bent, letter to George E. Hyde dated May 22, 1906, MS; Mokler, *Fort Caspar*, 32–33.

[13] Waring, *loc. cit.*, August 26, 1909.

[14] Fairfield, *loc. cit.*, 352–62.

under a bank near the river, fired and killed the Indian who had murdered his comrade. The men under Captain Lybe covered the body of Camp with their rifles, while Lord and two comrades brought the dead soldier in, thus preventing the body from being mutilated.[15]

When the action started, Private Waring got down from the top of the post, where he had been watching, and helped run the howitzer down to the river, but Major Anderson was unable to use it effectively because the soldiers and Indians were intermingled in one seething mass. All of the remaining available force of the garrison was sent to the relief of the sorely pressed party.

Jean Wilson, the newspaper correspondent for the Leavenworth *Daily Times*, told about how the rescue party opened a way for the retreat to the bridge:

> All seemed for one instant lost. At the first shot, Capt. G. [Greer] had dashed across, and maintained a most obstinate fight to hold the bridge and make way for our boys to get out. By hard fighting and pressing upon the savages, he managed to keep a way open for them to come into, and the only possible way for them to escape. His line advanced to good range of Lieut. Collins' party, but it was equally dangerous to our men as to the enemy, to fire there, they being mixed up all together. Lt. Collins gave the command, and his men charged, pistol in hand, to make, if possible, the bridge. On they came, the Indians with them. So determined seemed the savage foe, that had it not been for the unwavering courage of the brave men at the bridge, everything must have been lost. Lts. Drew and Bretney were on foot, and in the midst of the conflict. Capt. Greer was present everywhere, encouraging by command and presence, the men whose confidence he possessed and whom he knew would stand as long, and in any place he would direct. As in the battle of the 2nd of July, when he commanded, now he rode his favorite bay mare, Fanny, and, as then, though in the thickest of the fight, received no hurt. In twenty minutes from the time Lt. Collins left the bridge, his command, save four, reached it again. Nine were severely

[15] Mokler, *Fort Caspar,* 32.

wounded. The Lieutenant and four of his men were killed. The fight did not last over ten minutes. Every man who came back was more or less hurt, if not by arrows or shot, by bludgeons, clubs and bows.[16]

Lieutenant George M. Walker, the acting adjutant, said that the action lasted less than half an hour. All was therefore over before nine o'clock; this is verified by Private Waring, who said that, by this time, all was over on that part of the field. The late Alfred J. Mokler, who obtained his information from John C. Friend and the son of Lieutenant Bretney, said that the action started about seven-thirty and was over in an hour.[17]

The most complete account of the fight was given by Lieutenant Drew, who was watching through the spyglass on the roof of the station:

On reaching the top of the bluff, two Indians were seen by the detail at the top of the telegraph poles, a little over a quarter of a mile away, cutting the wires. As soon as they saw our men, they slid down the poles, mounted their horses and started for the back country as fast as the animals could carry them. Their mounts appeared to be very lame; they did not appear to make much headway, It looked like a soft snap to "take them in," and Lt. Collins ordered the boys to go for them before the Indians could reach their friends. This charge, of course, took them off the road and away from the sight of the river. The instant the last man disappeared from view, from behind the screen of willows west of the bridge, about 400 Cheyennes, on horseback, appeared, and with loud yells charged over the bottom lands and up on to the bluff in the direction which our men had gone. The instant they reached the top of the bluff, from behind every sand hill and out of every hollow, Indians appeared, and all with one object of charging on our detail and annihilating them before they could get back to the bridge and friends again. As soon as the detail realized the situation, they retraced their steps with all possible speed. It was not more than a couple of minutes before the Indians were all around them as thick as bees. In fact, so many of them were on all sides, that they did not dare to use their fire-

[16] Wilson, *loc. cit.,* August 30, 1865.
[17] Mokler, *Fort Caspar,* 33–34.

arms and bows and arrows for fear of shooting their own men but used their lances, tomahawks, and spears, and even tried to pull the boys off their horses by main force. The boys kept together in two ranks discharging their carbines with deadly effect into the crowd on their right and left; then not having time to reload, took their revolvers and kept up the shooting. A boy of about 17 belonging to Company I of the 11th Kansas, had what we call a "Muley" or "pepper box" revolver, the hammer being on the underside of the weapon, and by pulling the trigger the hammer would raise the piece, revolve to the next charge, and then the hammer would fall on the cap and fire it. A big Indian struck the boy over the head with his spear, trying to stun him, but the horses were moving so rapidly that it did not injure the boy very much. The youngster pointed his pepper box at the Indian; the Indian with a sardonic grin on his swarthy face, exclaimed, "Ugh. No Good," and tried to grab the boy off the horse. Just at that time the revolver went off and shot the Indian through the breast. His grin changed to a look of painful astonishment, as he fell forward on his pony's neck and wheeled out of the fight.

It did not take long for the detail to reach the edge of the bluff, and as soon as they got there the Indians on the right and left wheeled out of the way, and from the rear they poured out such a volley from their guns and revolvers that for a little while it reminded me of Wilson Creek or Prairie Grove battlefields. But our men were going very rapidly down hill and the Indians, in their alarm, fired so high that they hurt our men but very little, but did considerable harm to a lot of Sioux who were charging up to take the bridge. . . .

As soon as the Cheyennes came out of their ambush, all the men upon or near the bridge had run as fast as they could to help their comrades, who they knew would soon be striving to get back to the station. They had gotten about half way over the bottom land, when the detail came rushing down the hill, the Indians, seeing the footmen coming, were deterred from further pursuit. Lt. Britney and the party with him as soon as they saw the Cheyennes charge, turned from the bluff and ran to the bridge as fast as they could, and were just in time. From the deep gulch east of the bridge, about 500 Sioux had been lying in ambush, and as soon as the Cheyennes reached the top of the bluff, they came charging out to take the bridge, but seeing Britney and the men with him, and some reinforcements that came over to the bridge, pouring in the shots so lively from carbine and revolver, and the other Indians firing so high when shooting at our men who were coming over the bluff, and having the Sioux in exact range, a good many of the latter were hit, and it got so hot for them that they could not stand the pressure, but turned tail and fell back into the gulch again about as fast as they came out. If they had succeeded in their object of taking the bridge, they would probably have killed all of the balance of Collins' party and about fifteen or twenty others on the bottom land going to their relief and would then very likely have captured the station also. As soon as the Sioux were driven back from the bridge, the wounded men were sent to the station to have their wounds dressed and such other care as they required.[18]

Lieutenant Drew's statement that Collins left the road in order to pursue several Indians who had been cutting the telegraph wire is confirmed by the account of Lieutenant Walker, who claimed that this had been reported to him by men in Collins' command. Private Henry Lord of Company I said the same thing when he told of his part in the fight:

A few young Indians had been cutting the wires from the telegraph poles and now rode rapidly away. Collins had no idea of permitting them to escape so easily. He gave chase away from the trail and up over the sand hills to the north. Nothing could have happened to suit better the Indians' plan of attack, an opportunity to pick off a small troop and eventually seize the stockade and break the cordon of fortresses guarding the long trail. As Collins disappeared over the hill, 600 Cheyennes screened by willows some little distance up the stream, emerged from their cover and swept up the slope to envelope the band of cavalrymen. Lord and some other boys who had followed on foot across the river were on the point of moving out to support the troopers, when from downstream hidden in a gulch, a band of Sioux swarmed in a fierce rush to seize the bridge. The soldiers on foot repulsed this onset and held their position. As the Cheyennes emerged it was a signal for all the Indians to come out from behind every sand dune and from the shadow of every ravine. From every direction they converged on Collins and

[18] Drew, *loc. cit.*, April 27, 1882.

his little troop. The Indians were so eager to destroy they crowded in on the troops so closely they were unable to use their weapons effectively. . . . The desire to completely annihilate the cavalrymen caused the Sioux to abandon their attempt to capture the bridge and so they rode to join the mass of yelling, screaming red men. Lord and his comrades seized this opportunity to help Collins' men as far as possible. They ran upstream for a few hundred yards and formed an impromptu skirmish line. Dropping in the grass, their repeating arms swept the Indians' lines, which now resembled stampeding buffalo more than anything else. Dead warriors were catapulted from their frantic mounts. Wounded red men, their horses out of control and caught in the stampede, hastened to drop off while the ponies galloped riderless down into the narrow valley. The well aimed fire from the repeating arms of the soldiers on foot, all of whom were now marshaled to aid Collins' men, checked the tumultuous assault. The Indians withdrew to the crest of the hill out of reach of the long range rifles.[19]

The only accounts by men who were with Collins are those of Sergeant Isaac B. Pennock of Company I and Private Ferdinand Erhardt of Company K. Pennock did not say anything in his Diary about being led into a trap:

We crossed the bridge and got about one mile from camp when from N. E.—S. W. and every point of the compass the savages came. It appeared as if they sprung from the ground. They completely surrounded us. There was no other alternative. Death was approaching on every side in its most horrible form, that of the scalping knife tomahawk of the Indians. We turned and charged in the thickest of them, drawing our pistols and doing the best we could. It was a terrible ordeal to go through. It really was running the gauntlet for dear life after a terrible break neck race of ¾ miles we arrived at the bridge where our boys met us and to our support. In the charge we lost—five killed and twelve wounded. Lieut. Collins was killed. Everything was in full view of the station. Over 1,500 Indians were around our little party. The Indians suffered dreadfully as our pistols were pushed right against their bodies

[19] "Henry Lord of Dodge City Tells of the Battle of Platte Bridge," *loc. cit.*, 173–75.

and fired doing great execution. We were forced to come back. Every horse was wounded in one or more places. Four were killed. They now cut the wire both east and west.[20]

In later years Private Erhardt told about the fight but failed to say anything about following decoy Indians:

> There were 25 men of Cos. K and I, including myself. We started from the stockade under command of Lieut. Collins to the relief of the wagon train, and got perhaps a half a mile when, from ravines and behind hills, large numbers of redskins appeared and in a short time we were completely surrounded. Some of our boys had been killed and orders were given, "Retreat to the bridge," but that was not so easy. We were in close quarters: every man for himself. In the mixup the Indians quit firing, as they were hitting one another. About a dozen or more confronted me, and the nearest brave struck at me with his tomahawk. I dodged the blow and with my carbine close to his body I let him have the charge and he fell from his horse. There was no time to reload. I dropped my carbine on the sling to my side and drew my revolver, pointing it at one, then at another, then another, which had the effect to make them dodge right and left. I rode a good horse that obeyed the slightest touch of the rein with more than ordinary intelligence and a lively race followed, with a horde of savages on either side. It seemed to me that I was bringing up the rear and how to get through the ranks of Indians that had gathered between me and the bridge was a problem to be solved in a very few seconds. I was about to give up hope, when another trooper came along. They made a rush for him which left a gap through which my horse shot and on towards the bridge to safety. . . . Corporal Grimm came in with several arrows sticking in his back. . . . Had the Indians known that we were practically out of ammunition I might not be here to write this story.[21]

It would seem that if Lieutenant Collins had followed decoy Indians into a trap, this would have been indelibly impressed upon the minds of Sergeant Pennock and Private Erhardt, and they would have so stated. They belonged to a different regiment

[20] Pennock, *loc. cit.,* 19.

[21] Ferdinand Erhardt, "At Platte Bridge," *Kansas Scrap Book Biography E,* Vol. II, p. 225, reprinted from *National Tribune,* July 11, 1918.

and were free to tell the whole truth about the fight. Lieutenant Walker, Lieutenant Drew, and Private Henry Lord—the men who claim Collins fell into the trap—were not at the time in position to see what occured. It is difficult to believe that Collins with his three years' experience on the plains would have been fooled by such a commonplace and obvious device, but it is certain that for some reason he did turn away from the road. As Indians were seen from the post south of the road, it is probable that he, being higher up on the bluff, also saw them and turned northward to avoid them. When he turned away, they charged. George Bent said that all the Indians were on horseback watching Collins and his men going up the road into the trap, and that he could never understand why Collins did not see the heads of the Indians looking over the ridges. All the Indians said later that if Collins had gone half a mile farther along the road, every one of his command would have been killed. There was no signal; but when the Cheyenne Dog Soldiers under Big Horse charged from the river, the war party charged from the northeast from behind the hill, all converging on the little detachment.[22] When Collins was riding west along the edge of the bluff, he was approaching the trap which had been set for him; and if he had continued, his party would have been cut off from the fort. The Indians cutting the telephone wires could not have been decoys, because if Collins had, in fact, followed them, they would have led him out of the trap, enabling him to escape from the Indians along the river. It seems that whatever his motive was in turning north, this action saved his little command from total destruction. The fact that several warriors who had been cutting telegraph wires fled before his advance was quite accidental and not the reason for his departure from the road. There was little love lost between the Eleventh Ohio and the Eleventh Kansas,

[22] George Bent, letters to George E. Hyde dated May 10, 1905, and May 22, 1906, MS., Coe Collection, Yale University; November 10, 1915, MS., Denver Public Library.

and it is significant that none of the Kansas men made more than scant mention of Lieutenant Collins' heroism in the fight. George Bent said that he saw Collins on the gray horse pass by him with an arrow sticking in his forehead. He fell among the Indians, and Slow Bull captured the horse.[23]

When Collins' men were seen retreating in a column of twos, strung out in a line, Lieutenant Bretney and Captain Lybe recalled their men and fell back to some sand ridges near the bridge, which they held until all other troops had crossed. Twenty men were left to guard the bridge after the rest of the soldiers had gone to the stockade.[24]

Lieutenant Drew saw the aftermath of the retreat from his vantage point on the roof of the fort:

> The Indians were moving about on the bluff where the fighting was going on with Collins' party, threatening our men who had fallen, if there was any life left in any of them; and if dead, scalping and otherwise mangling their bodies in every conceivable manner. One of our men had fallen on the edge of the bluff, just as the boys were coming down the hill, fully a thousand yards from the bridge. An Indian rode up to his body and commenced shooting arrows into it. After firing four or five arrows the Indian dismounted, took his tomahawk and commenced to hack him with it. The boys at the bridge were very much excited about this, and some of them wanted to rush up and save the body from further mutilation, but under the circumstances it probably would have resulted in the killing or wounding of several more of our men, without doing any good, they were forbidden to undertake it. One of the boys put his gun to his shoulder and fired at the Indian, but the shot did not seem to disturb his equanimity in the least. Then Hank Lord remarked: "I believe I will take a whack at him." Elevating his sight to a thousand yards, he took deliberate aim and fired. The Indian had his hatchet raised at the time, and was about to strike it into the head of the dead soldier; but the bullet was too quick for him. It struck him in some vital part, for the hatchet dropped from his hand and he fell over on the ground. Pretty soon he managed to stagger to his feet,

---

[23] *Ibid.*   [24] Spring, *op. cit.,* 87.

68

and succeeded in getting on his pony and started away, but he was badly hurt and swayed from side to side on his pony. He was just about to fall off, when two Indians noticing his condition, rode up, one on each side, and supported him off the field. Very shortly after this we heard much loud talking among the Indians, who were gathered together in a large body on the bluff about three quarters of a mile from us. They seemed very much excited, and we expected they were making arrangements for another charge on the bridge, and we prepared ourselves for the onset, feeling very anxious as to what the result would be, but determined that should we be overwhelmed to sell our lives as dearly as possible. At this time, a half breed Snake Indian [Mitchell Lajeunesse], who lived in a tepee between the station and the bridge, and who had crawled up on the bluff to find out, if possible, what the trouble was, the number of Indians there and so forth, returned and reported that the Sioux and Cheyennes were having a big quarrel among themselves. The Cheyennes had charged the Sioux with being great cowards for not taking the bridge when they attempted it, thus failing to carry out the part of the program assigned to them. The Sioux retaliated with charging the Cheyennes with shooting a good many of their warriors when they fired down the hill at Lt. Collins' retreating party. The half breed stated that it might have the effect of breaking up the whole party, as each tribe declared that they would not coalesce with the other in the future, and were, moreover, just about ready to turn their weapons upon each other. The half breed's report relieved our anxiety, and we would have been very glad to have seen them commence hostilities against each other. It would have been a case of "dog eat dog," and we would have agreed to act in an impartial manner and not aid either side if they had consulted us in regard to it.[25]

The four men who had been killed with Lieutenant Collins were Privates George W. McDonald of Burlingame and Sebastian Nehring of Alma, both of Company I; Private George Camp of Pleasant Grove, of Company K; and Private Moses Brown, of Company H. Eight men were wounded, but none mortally. Private Henry W. Hill, Company I, of Burlingame, was listed

[25] Drew, *loc. cit.*, May 11, 1882.

as severely wounded; Private Jesse J. Playford, Company I, of Burlingame, was wounded in the neck with an arrow, which Private Henry Lord broke off and pulled through; Private Benjamin P. Goddard, Company I, of Shawnee, was wounded in the arm; and Privates George D. May, Company I, of Burlingame, and Harley L. Stodard, Company I, Undercook Harvey Craven, Company I, of Shawnee, and Private Andrew Baker, Company K, of Emporia, were listed as wounded. [26] Corporal Henry Grimm had an arrow in his back, which was pierced through after the feather end was cut off. The arrow in his spine remained there over four hours during the battle, since only one or two men could be spared to care for the wounded. He begged the doctor to take it out and not let him die with it in his back. Although he was not expected to recover, eight days later he was taken along on the march to Kansas. Grimm lived for thirty-nine years after being wounded, dying on January 3, 1904.[27]

The attempt to relieve the wagon train had been unsuccessful, and owing to the large number of Indians, estimated at from 2,500 to 3,000, the little detachment had been lucky to escape back to the post. It was now nine o'clock, and the wagon train could be expected at any time.

[26] The data on casualties are taken from the "Roster of the Eleventh Cavalry Regiment," *loc. cit.*

[27] Mokler, *Fort Caspar,* 32.

7

Lieutenant Walker's Skirmish

As THE SOLDIERS RETIRED across the bridge to the stockade, the pursuing Indians swam their ponies across the river and cut the telegraph wire on both sides of the station.

When Major Anderson called an officers' conference at 9:30 A.M., Lieutenant Bretney was grief-stricken and furious with anger because his best friend, Lieutenant Caspar Collins, had been killed. As Anderson refused to send word to the wagon train the night before, Bretney regarded the slaughter of the soldiers as useless. After hot words had been exchanged, Captain Greer, who had had trouble with Lieutenant Bretney on July 12, took up the quarrel. Greer was given a sound thrashing for his interference by Bretney, who was immediately placed under arrest by Major Anderson. He was not released until three o'clock that afternoon, but shortly after being placed under arrest, he sent word to Anderson that he would take seventy-five men and the howitzer and go to the relief of Custard and his men. The offer was rejected by Anderson on the ground that the men and howitzer were needed to protect the fort.[1]

Since the Indians had appeared in large numbers, Major Anderson determined to send to Deer Creek Station for reinforcements and ammunition. A party of Company I troops under

[1] Mokler, *Fort Caspar*, 33.

Lieutenant George M. Walker was sent out to repair the telegraph wire, which had been cut about one-half mile south of the river in the little valley two miles east of the post where the fighting had occurred the previous day. As the telegraph road ran half a mile south of the Platte, the wires were down north of where the action of the previous day had occurred and closer to the river. For about an hour there were no new developments at the station except that the Indians, by one means or another, tried to decoy some of the men away from the bridge.

> One Indian, on horseback, moved along a little beyond the edge of the bluffs, leading the gray horse which Lt. Collins had ridden. The gray acted very unwilling to be led and pulled back. Two of the Indians rode up to him and commenced whipping him, but the animal only curvetted about and did not get ahead very fast. Some of the boys took a few shots at the Indians, but the instant the flash from a gun was seen, the Indian would lean over on the opposite side of his pony, and all one could see would be his hand grasping the animal's mane, and his foot over its back. The instant the shot had passed, the Indian would straighten up again. The shots struck a pony or two, but we had no ammunition to spare for that sort of business, and orders were given to cease firing, save in case of an attack.
>
> As soon as the Indians saw that they could not draw us out in that manner, they commenced to call us all the vile names they could think of, using language they had picked up among the whites previously to the breaking out of the war, or had learned from the renegade whites among them.[2]

Meanwhile, the little detachment which had been sent to repair the wire ran into difficulties, which were described by the leader, Lieutenant Walker:

> About nine o'clock A.M. I was ordered to take 25 men and try to repair the line to the east. Owing to the condition of the horses, only a corporal and 16 men reported. Over a mile east of the station was a small creek, which, owing to the shape of its banks, had to be

[2] Drew, *loc. cit.*, May 11, 1882.

crossed at fords. The ford on the telegraph road was hidden from view of the station by a low mound. East of the creek was a low ridge half a mile wide and beyond lay the valley in which the herd had been attacked on the previous day. The ford was considered the danger point, as the Indian ford of the river was about a half mile north, and the Indians were congregated on the north bank.

Major Anderson ordered the Infantry captain to take his men to this mound to guard the ford until the repair force returned. He ordered me, in case the howitzer was fired, to drop all work and bring my men in at once. The Indian ford could be seen from the station, but not from the telegraph line east of the creek. We found nearly 1000 feet of wire had been destroyed in the valley near where the herd had been attacked. I directed one picked man to be sent north along the ridge to watch the Indian ford, and two, Chapel and Porter, to the high ground east.

The corporal and six men were sent to the east end of the break, and I started the other seven men stretching wire from the west end; and I went to the party on the east end, and was just dismounting when we heard the report of a howitzer, and at the same time our north picket fired his revolver. I signalled to the east picket and saw they were coming in, and ordered my men to mount. My attention was then called to the west squad, and I saw they were mounted and leaving us. I had a fleet horse, and used her speed, overhauling the men on the ridge and holding them in check until the corporal and his squad arrived and notified me that the pickets and all his men were in. We could not see the creek ford but did see that the infantry had abandoned the mound, leaving the danger point unprotected, and were on the double quick to the station. I saw some of my men near the ford, and believing our safety depended upon our being together, I again let out my horse and crossed the creek with the foremost; then wheeled and held the men until the corporal again notified me that the pickets and all men were in. A few Indians were in sight north of us within carbine range, and I had the men give them a volley from their carbines. We then moved forward in good order at a slow lope. When about a quarter of a mile from the mound my attention was called to the rear, where I saw Chapel coming in on foot, his horse lying in the road a few rods farther back, and two other men mounted in his rear, who proved to be Porter and Hilty, with a few Indians on fleet ponies behind and south of the men. Hilty was one of the corporal's squad, and had lagged behind to save his horse. I wheeled my men and started to their rescue. Chapel's horse had been killed by an Indian, and Porter and Hilty had each been speared in the back by Indians, who had rushed in from the north between the creek and the mound and struck the men from the rear. Porter fell from his horse within our lines, and was dead by the time a comrade could dismount and reach him. Hilty recovered and lived several years.[3]

When the cavalry troops retreated towards the post, several hundred young braves appeared on the trail, calmly awaiting their easy prey. The soldiers had no choice but to charge right through them, shooting as they charged.[4] Since the Indians were too close to use their weapons effectively, they rode alongside the men and sought to pull them from their saddles. When Private James A. Porter from Lyons County was lanced through the heart, Privates J. D. Meyers and Charles Waring grabbed him before he struck the ground and carried him to the post.[5] Farrier Joseph Hilty from Grasshopper fell forward on his horse's neck after being speared and clung to his horse until it carried him into the fort.[6] Several men of Company I were sent out on foot to aid the retreating men and arrived in time to help turn the Indians back. Several shots were fired from the howitzer. Sergeant Pennock wrote in his Diary that the detail had failed to repair the wire and that it had returned to the post at eleven-thirty o'clock. Captain Lybe, who had been in charge of the infantry support, resumed work on the breastworks after his return.[7]

[3] Walker, *loc. cit.*, 337–38.

[4] "Henry Lord of Dodge City Tells of the Battle of Platte Bridge," *loc. cit.*, 173–175.

[5] Waring, *loc. cit.*, August 26, 1909.

[6] As both Lieutenant Walker and Lieutenant Drew state that farrier Joseph Hilty was speared in the back during this skirmish, it would seem that the statement in the *Report of the Adjutant General of the State of Kansas, 1861–1865* that Hilty was wounded on July 25, 1865, is incorrect.

[7] Pennock, *loc. cit.*, 19; Spring, *op. cit.*, 89.

Lieutenant Drew, who remained at the post, gave a somewhat different version of the attempt to repair the telegraph line:

At the same time Walker's party left, the ten or twelve "galvanized soldiers," under command of their officer, were to go out about half a mile from the station and support the cavalry under Walker on their return to the station. If the Indians should develop any force that would interfere with repairs on the telegraph wires, a set of signals had been arranged by which Lt. Walker was to be notified if the Indians from the west were moving back . . . and interfering with the carrying out of his orders. The flag at the station was to be waved if the Indians were moving toward him, and should it develop that sufficient Indians were coming to frustrate his plans, the howitzer was to be fired, and at that, Lt. Walker was to bring his command back to the support of the others, and all would fall back to the station.

Walker arrived at the break in the telegraph wire, and then sent four men, Sergeant McDougal and Privates Porter, Hilty and Chappel, all of Company I, 11th Kansas Cavalry, about a quarter of a mile to the east to watch for Indians. The others went to work joining the wire, which was broken in several places.

Very soon after Walker's command left the station it was noticed that a large number of Indians . . . had commenced moving north, and it was but a short time before they were crossing a divide about a mile northeast of the station. We then knew they had observed the party leaving the station and were on their way to intercept them. The signal was thereupon given with the flag as soon as it was positive that enough of the savages had passed to be certain it would not do to delay any longer. The howitzer was also fired as a signal for the party to come in. As soon as the report was heard, the men dropped the wires, mounted their horses and then Walker, without waiting for the four men whom he had thrown out in advance, ordered the others in as fast as possible. The captain of the "galvanized troops," did not wait until the cavalry came up, but ordered his men back instanter. Some of the Company I boys had gone out on foot nearly to the point where the "galvanized troops," had been stationed. As soon as they heard the howitzer, they ran to where the relief had been stationed, and as soon as they passed the returning "galvanized troops," they cursed their captain for being a coward for leaving his post before the cavalry had overtaken him. The captain, however, paid no attention to their jeers, but pushed on to the station, although some of his men turned back to help the others. The cavalry advanced until they overtook the boys on foot, and then most of them turned to assist the four men on outpost from Walker's command, although Lt. Walker's horse got under such headway that it did not stop until it had carried him safely into the station, without his having fired a shot. About fifteen Indians had appeared out of a ravine and charged for the four men from the north side of the river. The men discharged their carbines, and then commenced to unload their revolvers. They were not noticing anything on the south. Several Indians came out of a ravine on the south close by, and before they were even observed, one of them had driven a spear into Porter's heart and he fell dead from his horse. Another Indian gave Hilty a stab with a spear which penetrated his lung. The savage withdrew his weapon as Hilty fell forward on his horse's neck. This Indian attempted to strike McDougal as he went by, but he was so close to the Sergeant that there was not room to use his weapon effectively. McDougal turned his head, and seeing that it was an Indian who was attempting to bore him with a spear, pressed his revolver against the Indian's body and pulled the trigger. The Indian fell from his horse, shot through the heart. It was the last cartridge McDougal had in his revolver, but it saved his life. By this time the boys on foot began to reach the Indians with their carbines, and as the Indians who had gotten into this skirmish were comparatively few in numbers, they did not press any closer.[8]

The wires were still down, and the little expedition had been a failure. The attempt to send a relief column to the wagon train that morning had been a failure also. One officer and five men had been killed, and many had been wounded. Ammunition was low, and there were but few serviceable horses left. Hordes of Indians were riding around the post. It was now eleven-thirty and the white tilts of the wagons should appear any time over the sandy ridge west of the station.

[8] Drew, *loc. cit.,* May 18, 1882.

8

Sergeant Custard's Wagon Train Fight

DURING LIEUTENANT WALKER'S UNSUCCESSFUL ATTEMPT to repair the telegraph line east of Platte Station, Sergeant Custard's little party was approaching the post from the west on the telegraph road, unaware of the fighting. They had crossed the high divide east of the telegraph patrol about nine o'clock and were still eight miles from Platte Station. After resting the mules, they resumed the journey down the east slope of the divide and then up one of the longest and steepest grades on the Oregon Trail, which led up between two mounds forming a saddle gap four miles west of the station. The mules were rested again after the long climb. The men could not see the post from here, for it was hidden behind a bluff; and the soldiers in the vicinity of the station did not see the wagons coming down over the gap, as they were occupied with Lieutenant Walker's skirmish and narrow escape toward the east. Custard followed down the steep grade, winding around among the sand hills on the bluffs above the river. One branch of the road angled southeast to a camping place at the river bend then ran along the bottomland to the fort. As Custard chose the route up over the bluffs instead of following the easier route, where he might have been ambushed, he was undoubtedly on the alert for Indians. As he came up the gradual slope of the last little ridge, a mile and a quarter from his goal, about eleven-thirty, one of the soldiers at the fort saw the canvas tops of the wagons and sang out, "There comes the train:"[1]

The Indians saw it at the same time and, getting on their ponies, urged them at their fastest pace towards the little caravan. The howitzer at the fort was aimed at the largest body of Indians and the fuse was cut for three seconds. When discharged, the shell exploded in mid-air, doing no damage. Another shell was inserted with a larger fuse but also exploded before reaching the Indians.[2] The shots served to give warning to the wagon train. When Sergeant Custard heard them, he detailed Corporal Shrader to take four men and ride ahead to see what the firing was about. Sergeant Custard had at least five horses with the train, as all accounts refer to the "horses" of the advance party. The probabilities are that these men were already mounted, since "he put out flankers from his small party."[3]

The five men rode a quarter of a mile in advance, and the wagons started down over the ridge at a fast gait in a headlong dash for the post.[4] For about half a mile the ground was almost level, forming a little plateau among the sand hills above the river. The sides of the bluff concealed the attacking Indians, who were not seen until they suddenly appeared simultaneously in the northeast, east, and south, coming up onto the plateau. Corporal Shrader tried to turn back to the wagon train, but it was too late. Indians riding up a ravine from the south cut him off, and his only chance was to make a dash for the river about half a mile distant.[5] Reaching the river in safety, the men plunged in on their horses and swam across, the attention of the mass of Indians being directed to the larger force with the wagons. One man held his pistol above his head so the powder would not get

---

[1] Drew, *loc. cit.,* May 11, 1882.
[2] *Ibid.*
[3] "Military History of the Eleventh Kansas Volunteer Cavalry," *loc. cit.,* 213.
[4] Drew, *loc. cit.,* May 11, 1882.
[5] *Ibid.*

78

wet. Three men in advance reached the opposite river bank; two of them turned toward the fort, but Private Edwin Summers, seeing a band of about fifteen Indians approaching from that direction to cut them off, refused to go with the others and headed his horse southwest towards the mountain. He was last seen near the foothills, closely pursued by several warriors.[6]

When the feet of Corporal Shrader's horse touched the south bank of the river, Shrader decided to abandon it and slipped from its back. Just then the horse of his companion. Private James Ballau, was shot under him, and Ballau sprang from his own horse and placed his hand on Shrader's horse, exclaiming, "My God, Jim, what shall we do? We shall all be killed!"

As these words were spoken, a bullet struck him, and he fell dead on the brink of the river. His body was never found, and it was supposed that it had floated down the river.[7]

Shrader hastily climbed up the riverbank and ran to catch up with the other two men. About halfway to the post, they encountered the band of Indians. During the little skirmish that followed, the leader of the band, Left Hand, brother of the famous Cheyenne chief Roman Nose, was shot through the head with a pistol as he rode out of the river. Another Indian was killed here; and while the others gathered about their fallen leader, the fugitives were able to reach a clump of sagebrush along a deep ravine, where they hid and abandoned their horses. While concealed in the ravine at the river bend half a mile southwest of the post, the three survivors examined their ammunition and, finding some of their cartridges wet from their ducking in the river, proceeded to load them with dry powder.[8]

Presently Shrader saw one Indian's head above a gopher or ant hill, and raised up with his carbine aimed to pick him off, when a

[6] Pennock, *loc. cit.*, 19.

[7] "The Platte Bridge Fight," Oskaloosa *Independent,* July 8, 1865, as reprinted in Topeka (Kansas) *Capital,* July 3, 1882.

[8] *Ibid.*

ball from another direction came so close to his head as to knock him down. His companions asked if he was hurt, and he replied: "No, I guess only stunned."

Soon after the three crept off on their hands and knees and succeeded in placing a ridge between themselves and the savages, and then cautiously made toward the fort. They saw no Indians until they passed over one or two more ridges, and then looking back noticed a number of the redskin sentinels keeping guard around the sage brush, evidently not yet aware of their escape.

About this time a body of men from the fort came to their rescue, and the three in the lead dismounting, and placing three weary Kansans on their ponies, bade them make for the fort while they followed on foot. All arrived at the stockade in safety.

The names are Shrader, Swain and Smith. As already stated Mr. Shrader resides near this city [Oskaloosa, Kansas]. Mr. Swain lives about eight miles east of here, but where Mr. Smith resides at present, we are not advised.[9]

As the three men ran out of the ravine toward the fort, fifteen or twenty Indians came out of the same ravine at a point nearer the river and tried to head them off. The soldiers from the fort called to the men to come down a gully, where they would be covered by their fire. In this manner the Indians were forced to keep under cover, permitting all the men to run to the stockade, where they arrived about four o'clock and were given a hearty welcome by the men of the garrison. All that saved them was their good sense in abandoning their horses and the desire of most of the Indians to ignore them and plunder the wagon train.[10]

There is complete confusion among the accounts regarding the names of the men and the places where each was killed. Lieutenant Walker, who was watching the men through his field glasses, said that Private William West's horse was killed in the river and the rider was last seen on the south bank of the stream refusing to go with the others. Mrs. Spring makes the statement

[9] *Ibid.*
[10] Drew, *loc. cit.*, May 11, 1882.

that the body of Private William West was never found,[11] probably on the strength of the Walker account. Some claimed that Ballau was killed south of the river, between the crossing and the post, giving the impression that there were three men killed out of an advance party of six. Shrader, upon his visit to Casper in 1926 at the age of eighty-four, stated that it was Private James Ballau who was shot on the riverbank and Private Edwin Summers who was buried one mile south of the river, making no mention of Private William West.[12] Since Shrader claimed that he buried Summers, it would seem that Summers was the trooper who refused to go with the others and was overtaken by Indians and killed near the foothills. Although Ballau was shot on the river bank and his body was never found, that night Captain Huntoon reported him killed as the incident had occurred in the presence of Corporal Shrader. It is believed that Shrader's account is the most authentic. In spite of his advanced years, he surely must have remembered the identities of the soldier he had buried and the man whose body he had searched for along the south bank of the river. That there were only two of the party killed is confirmed by the fact that there were twenty bodies found on the Custard site. If Private William West had been killed with Shrader, there would have been only nineteen there. During the Casper visit, Shrader also stated that two horses had been killed, so they abandoned the third one and proceeded on foot, arriving at the stockade about two-thirty that afternoon.

Back on the hill Sergeant Custard had driven too far to take position on the little mounds where he had crossed the divide,[13] for the Indians were coming fast, and he had to corral his wagons immediately. South of the road was a slight hollow about two hundred yards across and the same distance east of the ridge,

11 Spring, *op. cit.*, 94.
12 Mokler, *Fort Caspar*, 43–44.
13 Walker, *loc. cit.*, 338–39.

He swung the lead wagon southward across the hollow and up onto the rim, while the next two empty wagons followed him but stopped down in the hollow, leaving the lead wagon isolated in an exposed position. The second and third wagons were corralled, one behind the other, about sixty yards short of the first wagon, while the fourth remained 140 yards north and a little west of the two in the hollow. The rear wagon must have been far behind since it stopped on the north edge of the hill south of the road. It might be surmised that the occupants, upon hearing the firing when coming over the ridge, left the road in an attempt to cut across to the corral but had to stop on top of the hill to defend themselves. The men in the two rear wagons must have abandoned them and raced to join the others in the hollow, while those in the lead wagon undoubtedly ran back down, so that all the men fought from the two wagons in the corral. The watchers at the station could see the men try to corral the wagons and said that they did not succeed very well.[14] The wagon on the south rim of the hollow was visible, while the two in the hollow, being close together, probably appeared as one wagon. The rear wagon on the north end of the ridge was the other one seen, while the fourth wagon, which had stopped a short distance south of the road, was not visible from the station. George Bent said that Wolf-Coming-Out, who was the first Indian on the scene, told him that the frantic mules were milling around, the soldiers having cut them loose from the wagons. One of the Indians caught the bell mare and led her away, with all the other mules following.[15]

As the yelling and whooping Indians charged the wagon corral from the east, the soldiers grabbed their carbines and poured in volley after volley, shooting many of the warriors from their ponies. By their courage and presence of mind, the men weath-

[14] Pennock, *loc. cit.*, 19.

[15] Grinnell, *op. cit.*, 224; George Bent, letter to George E. Hyde dated November 10, 1915, MS., Denver Public Library.

ered the sudden assault upon them. After the first headlong charge the Indians withdrew, while the men piled bedding, sacks of corn, and boxes under the wagons, forming a barricade. Most of the men fought from under the wagons, but four were inside one wagon, firing through holes cut in the canvas cover. The Indians were now completely surrounding the wagons and again charged, but were once more driven back. The soldiers fought with wonderful skill and resolution. These seasoned veterans had faced death on too many battlefields to be frightened at it in whatever terrible guise it might come.[16] "The foe charged time and again upon the wagons, and as often seemed to be repulsed. That they met with a desperate resistance, could be seen by their repeated charges and movement in circle at a considerable distance from the wagons."[17]

Sergeant Pennock, who was watching from the fort, noted in his Diary:

> All this we could plainly see from the station, but we could do nothing for them. "H" and "D" detachments corralled, or tried to corral their wagons, but did not succeed very well. We could see the Indians in swarms charge down on our boys when they would roll volley after volley into them, it seemed as though the boys were in a strong position, twenty in all being their number.[18]

Lieutenant Walker stated that he saw the smoke from the men's carbines as the Indians charged into them, and after the volleys the Indians scattered "like a flock of birds shot into."[19] The Indians had a few antiquated rifles with which they probably killed several of Custard's men, but their main weapon was the bow and arrow. Having a great fear of carbines fired by soldiers on foot, they remained concealed behind the bluffs, rocks, and sagebrush. Company I was camped near the bank of the

---

[16] "Military History of the Eleventh Kansas Volunteer Cavalry," *loc. cit.*, 213.

[17] Wilson, *loc. cit.*, August 30, 1865.

[18] Pennock, *loc. cit.*, 19.

[19] Walker, *loc. cit.*, 338.

river east of the bridge, but did not dare approach near enough to give the Indians a shot from the north side of the river.[20]

The warriors, finding that it was certain death to get within range of the deadly carbines of the soldiers, resorted to typical Indian strategy, and the fight settled down to a long-distance siege. The soldiers were on the alert, and every Indian who exposed himself was fired upon. Sometimes a single rifle report would come from the hollow, again two or three shots would be heard in quick succession, and then, after an ominous silence, a volley would rumble and rattle over in the hollow to be followed by a painful silence.[21]

From a small branch ravine with bluff banks southwest of the corral, the Indians dug trenches with knives and tomahawks and commenced a gradual approach in such numbers as would enable them to overwhelm the soldiers when they got close enough. Places were scooped out large enough to aim a rifle through. They carried logs and rocks to the vicinity and rolled them forward, making a movable breastwork, from behind which they fired their guns and arrows into the open, unprotected west side of the little corral.[22] The fire of the doomed men became slower and slower as they watched the piles of sand come closer and closer. As time wore on, they must have looked anxiously down towards the station, momentarily expecting troops to come to their relief. Finally, after firing a volley, the Indians seemed to spring out of the ground all around the corral with savage yells of exultation. There were a number of shots fired; and, after a hand-to-hand struggle of short duration, there were more savage yells from Indians in all directions. The garrison at the post knew well what had happened, but they knew also that the brave men had compelled their enemies to pay dearly for their victory.[23]

[20] *Ibid.*, 339.

[21] Coutant, *op. cit.*, 475.

[22] "Military History of the Eleventh Kansas Volunteer Cavalry," *loc. cit.*, 213; Spring, *op. cit.*, 92.

[23] Drew, *loc. cit.*, May 25, 1882; "Military History of the Eleventh Kansas

George Bent, the French-Cheyenne, who was with the Indians, described the attack on the government wagons of six mules each, which occurred about noon:

> While we were all standing on the hill talking about the fight Indians hollered to us that they were signalling on horses that whites were in sight up the river. We all jumped on our horses and rode up the road in plain view of the soldiers at the bridge. This must have been a grand sight for them as all the Indians were running up the river toward the Government train that Casper Collins was going out to meet that morning when he was killed. This was about five miles from the bridge where the train coralled in sand hills next to the river. When I got there I looked down the road as far as I could see the Indians were still coming and a lot of them were already fighting the soldiers. Just as my party were riding up a lot of mules came running towards us. Indians were behind them. The soldiers got under the wagons and used their bedding sacks of corn and miscellaneous boxes for breastworks as they had time to do all this before the Indians got all around them. They seen Indians all around Bridge and from where Collins men were laying from where they first came up the hill. They could see plainly to the bridge as it was level to the bridge. They selected good place to fight from. It was kind of a basin. This basin was about a hundred yards wide each way as I took good look at it after the soldiers were all killed. 22 soldiers were killed in this party, one driver swam across and got away. This man shot Roman Nose's brother two Indians swam across after him he only had pistol buckled around his head when he swam the river. He hid in brush after he crossed and Roman Nose's brother ran into him without seeing him and he shot him through the head. Nobody did not know he was killed for some time as everybody was busy with the soldiers fighting them. They had good deal of stock with them. 8 Indians were killed in this battle, 4 soldiers were in the wagons that done good shooting. All the wagons had covers on them and these 4 men cut holes in the sheets to shoot through so much firing was going on the Indians did not know that they were in the wagons for some time. The Indians were shooting at those under the wagons. Someone spoke up smoke coming from

Volunteer Cavalry, *loc. cit.*, 213; George Bent, letter to George E. Hyde dated May 3, 1906, MS, Coe Collection, Yale University; Coutant, *op. cit.*, 475.

the wagons as he seen it plain. He pointed the wagon then the Indians shot at this wagon several times lot of them together Wolf Tongue (twins) Roman Nose in fact several brave warriors said all to get ready that they were going to ride around the wagons and empty the soldiers' guns. Then those on foot to charge up against the wagons. I stood up and seen these warriors with their war bonnets and shields on as they rode around the wagons at first good many shots came from under the wagons and once three or four shots from the wagon. Then all the Indians made warwhoop and charged from all sides. Then I ran down there which was only 50 yards they were shooting the soldiers under the wagons and those in the wagon three of them had been killed one soldier they threw out of the wagon and killed him on the ground. After this fight we all came back to where we all stayed that night as we had left our packs, ponies and saddles as Indians ride bareback in all fights. Next morning good many small war parties started again in different directions biggest party started for home. I was with this party.

The Cheyennes killed here were Young Wolf, High Wolf, Young Bear, Old Bull Hair, Stray Horse, Spit, and Roman Nose's brother. [24]

George Bird Grinnell said that among the Indians who had recently joined the large war party was a village of Brûlé Sioux, but only a portion of them were present at the fight at Platte Bridge.[25]

Lieutenant Drew watched the fight from the roof of the station with the aid of a large spyglass and had a good view of what was going on at the train:

It had stopped on a side-hill, and with the three wagons the men had formed three sides of a square, with one facing up the hill to the north, one east, one south, but the west side open. The first Indians who came to the scene of action charged right onto the train, but they were repulsed. As others arrived they again made a charge, but were again driven back. After this, for a long time there did

---

[24] George Bent, letter to George E. Hyde dated May 3, 1906, MS, Coe Collection, Yale University. While Bent says that there were eight Cheyennes killed, he lists only seven.

[25] Grinnell, *op. cit.*, 224.

THE SUPPLY TRAIN

From a drawing by Frederic Remington in Harper's Weekly,
December 6, 1890

YOUNG MAN AFRAID OF HIS HORSES

*Courtesy of the Denver Public Library
Western Collection*

GEORGE BENT and
His Cheyenne Wife, Magpie

Courtesy of George E. Hyde

not seem to be much action going on. Every once in a while we could see a cloud of smoke from the wagons, or from the side hill below the wagons, which showed that the fight was still in progress, but we could not tell with what result, though we noticed that the puffs of smoke from the hillside on the south were gradually getting closer and closer, and we felt that the end could not be far off. Never in all our service as soldiers had we experienced anything like this before. To know that about twenty of our comrades, with whom for nearly three years, we had been soldiering in the south, were now within two and one half miles of us, surrounded by an overwhelming number of savage enemies determined on their destruction, and we not able to do anything for their relief, was heartrending. Some of us went to Major Anderson and requested that forty or fifty of us be allowed to volunteer and go out on foot to attempt a rescue, but the Major, while feeling deeply for the brave fellows who were making such a heroic fight against such terrible odds, realized that an attempt at relief by anyone who started from the bridge force would doubtless mean the destruction of the entire party, in which event it would be an easy matter for the Indians to have taken the station and massacred all who were left. At that time we thought the Major too cautious but since then, knowing what the Indians did to Fetterman's party the next year near Fort Phil Kearny, and later to the gallant Custer and his brave men at Little Big Horn, we are satisfied that the Major's decision was a wise one, and that by it alone are any of us left alive today. . . . We observed that the firing had ceased at the train. Soon after, a large smoke arose, and we saw that the wagons were burning fiercely. We then knew that the fighting was all over, and that the brave men who had so well defended themselves, were all dead. They had made a gallant fight for four hours, but had been overpowered at last. The Indians hung about the place watching the wagons burn, until nearly nightfall, and then a great many of them moved back to the bluffs north of the river.[26]

Most of the eyewitnesses agreed that the fight at the wagon train had lasted about four hours.[27] Those who stated that it started at eleven o'clock said that it ended at three, while Sergeant Pennock said it was all over at four o'clock, having begun

[26] Drew, *loc. cit.,* May 18, 1882.
[27] Wilson, *loc. cit.,* August 30, 1865.

some time after Lieutenant Walker had returned to the post at eleven-thirty.[28] As the Sergeant was in the habit of noting the time of events all through his Diary, his statements are probably the most reliable.

From the account of Charles Whitehead,[29] who claimed to have been with the telegraph patrol at Red Buttes, it would appear that Custard, after being warned of the presence of many Indians about Platte Station, went on in reckless disregard for his own safety and that of his men. Lieutenant Bretney, in his earlier statements to Lieutenant Walker, said that he saw no Indians while coming to the station and was surprised when told about the fighting of the day before. This is confirmed by the account of Lieutenant Drew.[30] It should be remembered that Bretney had the right by seniority to order Custard to accompany him but did not do so. Bretney and Whitehead were in the rival Eleventh Ohio Cavalry, and, as Custard was dead, he could not give his side of the story. The army considered a force of twenty-five men strong enough to travel in safety almost anywhere on the road from Laramie to South Pass.[31] Custard had been ordered to take the supply train to Platte Station by noon of the twenty-sixth, and was just following orders. It should be noted that no criticism, official or otherwise, has been directed at Custard for his conduct other than the alleged statements of Bretney and Whitehead. Indians had been harassing the Oregon Trail posts for months; and if there were some at Platte Station, it was nothing new or unexpected. As all but a few of the Indians had remained concealed, there was no reason to suspect that such a large war party was near the post.

The men of the Eleventh Kansas Cavalry came west fresh from triumphs over the Rebels with the feeling that they were

28 Pennock, *loc. cit.*, 19.

29 Whitehead, *loc. cit.*, 288–92.

30 Drew, *loc. cit.*, April 27, 1882; Walker, *loc. cit.*, 336.

31 Wilson, *loc. cit.*, August 30, 1865.

invincible. While Sergeant Custard had been in the thick of the fighting in Missouri and Arkansas, he had had only one experience fighting Indians. On May 20, three to five hundred warriors had surrounded and attacked Three Crossings Station. After some fighting they left about five o'clock, taking along one pony which was grazing outside the stockade.[32] There had been no casualities, and the hit-and-run tactics of the Indians must have confirmed the Sergeant's belief that the Indians were poor fighters. While he should not be held responsible for the disaster, Sergeant Custard, like General Custer and Lieutenant Colonel Fetterman, had a supreme contempt for the Indians and did not realize the prowess in war of the Sioux and Cheyennes.

[32] Pennock, *loc. cit.,* 6.

9

Death in the Sand Hills

AN HOUR AFTER THE WAGON TRAIN WAS BURNED, a detachment of men, including Lieutenant Bretney, who had been released, and Privates William Worrell, Tom Sinclair, and John C. Friend of the Eleventh Ohio Cavalry, Company G, went across the bridge to bring back the bodies of Lieutenant Collins and those who had been killed with him.[1] As they went along the bluff to the place where Collins had turned to rescue the wounded trooper, they found a body, which they lifted and laid across Friend's horse. Just as another body was found nearby, the Indians appeared with the evident intention of cutting off the bold riders, and the detachment hastily retired to the fort.[2] The body brought into the post was probably that of Private Moses Brown of Company H, because that night his commanding officer, Captain Joel Huntoon at Horseshoe Station, reported his death.[3] In the muster roll of Company H, Eleventh Kansas Cavalry (August 31, 1865), opposite the name of Moses Brown is an asterisk referring to a footnote at the bottom of the page which reads, "Killed with party sent to relief of wagon train," over the signa-

[1] Coutant, *op. cit.*, 473.

[2] *Ibid.*

[3] Telegram dated July 26, 1865, from J. Huntoon to Lawrence (Kansas) *Tribune,* August 3, 1865.

Jean Wilson, in his article in the Leavenworth (Kansas) *Daily Times,* Auture of Captain Joel Huntoon. That Brown's body was brought in on the evening of July 26 is confirmed by the fact that the body of George Camp had been brought in during the fight and those of Sebastian Nehring and George W. McDonald were not recovered until the afternoon of the next day, July 27. Private Moses Brown, one of the children of J. Brown, born in Marysville, Missouri, was only eighteen when he enlisted as an unmarried farmer from Kaw Township.

Near one of the bodies a piece of paper was lying which one of the men picked up. From its appearance it was torn out of a pocket diary or an account book. It was written about as follows:

"I was taken prisoner about seven months ago at Le Bonte Station. You must be careful or you will be killed. There are between three and four thousand Indians here, and about another thousand expected here in a day or two. They belong to the Cheyenne, Sioux, and Arapahoe, with a few Commanches and Blackfeet. You killed one of their principal chiefs belonging to the Cheyennes yesterday, and they swear they will have a terrible revenge upon you for it. The intentions are to clean out all the stations on this road and then go onto the Ft Collins road and clean that out. I shall escape from them if I can."

I do not remember the name signed to it, but it was evidently some person with the Indians who was feeling friendly towards us. Some of the 11th Ohio men thought it was a man who belonged to one of their companies and who was supposed to have deserted at the time mentioned at Le Bonte station. A good many of the 11th Ohio Cavalry had been recruited from the rebel soldiers who had gone into Ohio on the celebrated Morgan raid, and after their capture preferred enlistment in the United States Army to fight Indians in preference to remaining in military prisons in the north until the war should end, or until they could be exchanged. Most of them made good, faithful soldiers, but some of them were exceptionally hard cases, deserting and joining the Indians, and helping them in their warfare against the whites; and what the Indians didn't know of devilment, these renegades taught them.[4]

gust 30, 1865, said that at sunset on the day of the battle, two men killed in the "first fight" were buried. These were probably Privates Camp and Brown.

[4] Drew, *loc. cit.,* May 18, 1882.

The death of Private James Ballau was also reported on the evening of July 26 by Captain Huntoon.[5]

As some demonstration by the Indians was expected that night, Lieutenant Bretney was placed in command of his Eleventh Ohio troopers, who were detailed as picket guard. Other guards about the post were doubled and extra vigilance was kept. Just about midnight a few of the Indians prowled about the post, but the guards were on the alert and fired at them. They responded with a few arrows but made no further attack. A picket shot a calf in the darkness when it failed to halt upon command.[6]

As the telegraph wires were cut and it was necessary to send for reinforcements and ammunition immediately, Major Anderson hired Mitchell and Noel Lajeunesse (also known as "Ciminau" or "Seminoe"), sons of a Shoshoni woman and a French father, the government scouts who lived in the tipis between the stockade and the river, to carry orders to Deer Creek Station, twenty-eight miles to the east. Lieutenant Hubbard, who commanded Company K during the illness of Captain Allen, was ordered to bring his company with extra ammunition to reinforce the garrison at Platte Station and to telegraph headquarters at Fort Laramie reporting the action of July 26.[7] One of the scouts was mounted on an Indian pony noted for its speed and endurance which had been captured that day from an Indian chief.[8] They were paid $150 each and left the post about ten o'clock, riding directly towards the mountain, where they turned eastward along a trail to Deer Creek.[9] The scouts arrived at their destination early the next morning, and Lieutenant Hubbard, after reporting the situation by wire to headquarters, started about six o'clock on a forced march to Platte Station with fifty

---

[5] Telegram dated July 26, 1865, from J. Huntoon to Lawrence (Kansas) *Tribune,* August 3, 1865.

[6] Spring, *op. cit.,* 93 ; Drew, *loc. cit.,* May 25, 1882.

[7] Mokler, *Fort Caspar,* 16; Drew *loc. cit.,* May 25, 1882.

[8] Drew, *loc. cit.,* May 25, 1882.

[9] *Ibid;* Spring, *op. cit.,* 92.

men of Company K and five thousand rounds of ammunition.[10]

At Horseshoe Station, Captain Joel Huntoon, upon intercepting the bad news, wired a dispatch to the Kansas *Tribune* which appeared in the August 3, 1865, issue of that newspaper:

> HORSE SHOE STATION, JULY 26.
>
> EDITOR TRIBUNE:—Please publish the casualties in detail from Co. H, 11th K.V.C., escorting a train which was burned by the Indians near "Red Buttes." The killed were Moses Brown, Jas. Ballau. Missing Sergt. Custard, Privates Jesse E. Autrain, Wm. Brown, Geo. Brown, Geo. Heath, Angus Hoppe, John Houston, Wm. Long, Ferdinand Schaffer, Saml Sproul, Wm. West, Thos. Young. The missing were probably killed having defended the train until their ammunition was expended. Co. H is from Shawnee.
>
> J. HUNTOON
> *Capt. Co. H. 11 K.V.C.*

In this telegram one "Geo. Brown" is listed as missing, but there was no soldier of that name in Company H or in the whole Eleventh Kansas Cavalry Regiment. In a telegram dated July 28 from Captain Huntoon to the editor of the Leavenworth *Daily Conservative,* appearing in the July 29 issue of that newspaper, the name of "Geo. Brown" is omitted from the casualty list. The original inclusion of that name was apparently an error.

In response to the wire for reinforcements, four squadrons of the Sixth Michigan Cavalry under Colonel J. Kidd and five squadrons under Captain Creevy were ordered to make a forced march from Fort Laramie to Platte Station.[11]

On the morning of July 27 there were only a few Indians in sight on the bluffs around the post, and parties of them were seen going off in a northwesterly direction all morning. By noon the last of them had disappeared. As the supply of ammunition was low, Lieutenant Walker was directed to get all the powder and lead that the ranchmen had and set the men to making cartridges. Lieutenant Walker said later that if the garrison had not

[10] Drew, *loc. cit.,* May 25, 1882.
[11] Spring, *op. cit.,* 93.

been so short of ammunition, a greater effort would have been made to rescue the wagon train.[12]

That afternoon a detachment which included Sergeant Pennock and Privates Waring and S. H. Fairfield was sent across the bridge with an ambulance to gather up the remaining bodies of Lieutenant Collins' party. They found Private Sebastian Nehring of Company K with his arms bound to his body with telegraph wire, his hands and feet cut off, his tongue and heart cut out, and other horrible mutilations. Sixty-five arrows were counted in his body, which was pinned to the ground with a long spear. The body of Private George W. McDonald of Company I was found stripped and mutilated, with several arrows in it.[13] According to Private John C. Friend, the search party spread out fan-shaped over the hills and worked north, looking for the body of Lieutenant Collins. After about an hour it was found by a man who had gone north from the place of the encounter. There were twenty-four arrows in the body. Collins was stripped naked, the back part of his head knocked off, brains taken out, heart and bowels taken out, feet and hands cut off, and the body tied up with telegraph wire. The remains were wrapped in a blanket, placed in the ambulance, taken to the post, and buried in the soldiers' cemetery with military honors.[14]

Private Fairfield said the body was found half a mile from the bridge;[15] Lieutenant Walker stated that it was located one mile northeast of the bridge, but on his map showed it about one mile northwest of the post at the foot of the divide.[16] John C. Friend, while attending a celebration in Casper on July 5, 1920, said that all the old landmarks were gone and that the

---

[12] Walker, *loc. cit.*, 339.

[13] Pennock, *loc. cit.*, 20; Waring, *loc. cit.*, August 26, 1909; Fairfield, *loc. cit.*, 359.

[14] Mokler, *Fort Caspar*, 34.

[15] Fairfield, *loc. cit.*, 359.

[16] Walker, *loc. cit.*, 357.

body of Caspar Collins was found two to four miles north of the fort.[17] Mrs. Spring states that the body was found early in the morning of July 28 by the Ohio boys about three miles from where the fight took place, near the creek which was later named for him. Telegraph wire had been wrapped around the body, which had been dragged some distance.[18] As Mrs. Spring derived her information personally from Lieutenant Bretney and John C. Friend, it would seem that her version is the most authentic. The little creek, formerly known as "Dry Creek," where Collins' body was found, was renamed "Casper Creek," and the city which sprang up later near there was named "Casper" in his honor. The mountain to the south, which had always been called "Black Hills," was given the name of "Casper Mountain." His remains were disinterred on March 19, 1866, and sent to his home in Hillsboro, Ohio.[19]

The place where the fight occurred was about half a mile west and half a mile north of the bridge, or several hundred yards north of the present cemetery marker. Two of the men who were killed with Collins (probably Nehring and McDonald) were buried in this little cemetery plot on the edge of the bluff half a mile west of the post and several hundred yards north of the river, at the point where Collins' party stampeded down into the bottomland.[20] As Camp and Brown had been taken to the post, they were probably buried in the post cemetery several hundred yards east of the fort. In 1898 the river changed its course and washed away the bank on the north side, exposing the remains of some soldiers buried under the bluff. These were removed to

---

[17] Mokler, *Fort Caspar,* 70.

[18] Spring, *op. cit.,* 93–94.

[19] Mokler, *Fort Caspar,* 34–35.

[20] *Ibid.* A sketch of this little cemetery appears in Mokler, *Transition of the West.* As Privates Camp and Brown were brought into the post and buried there the day of the battle, the bodies buried in this cemetery were those of Privates Nehring and McDonald, whose bodies were badly mutilated and not recovered until the day after the battle.

Highland Memorial Park and the next year moved by the War Department to Fort D. A. Russell, near Cheyenne, Wyoming.[21] It would be difficult to find relics of this running fight since none of the carbines or pistols used by the soldiers fired metallic cartridges. The old road which ran along the river bottom westward from the bridge is now covered by the present highway and an industrial plant, while the site of the first encounter is covered with gravel pits.

About three o'clock in the afternoon Lieutenant Hubbard arrived with his fifty men of Company K and ammunition, and was cheered lustily. As soon as they had rested a few minutes, they, along with a detachment of Company I, started on the trail

[21] Mokler, *Fort Caspar,* 60–65. Information concerning the location of reburials of soldiers from Platte Bridge in the Fort Francis E. Warren Cemetery (D. A. Russell) has been furnished by Layle B. Nelson, cemeterial officer, Francis E. Warren Air Force Base, Wyoming, in a series of letters to the author. Graves numbered 252 through 264, a total of thirteen, in Section C of the cemetery contain the remains of soldiers having no markings, numbers, or other identification. However, according to a pencil notation on the records, these were from Casper, Wyoming, and were probably the thirteen bodies which were disinterred and shipped to the cemetery by H. M. Brown, as stated in Mokler's *Fort Caspar,* 59–60.

George W. Wallace, Jr., staff sergeant, Mortuary, U.S.A.F. cemetery, of Francis E. Warren Air Force Base, Wyoming, in a letter of April 8, 1963, to the author, has furnished additional information regarding other reburials, as indicated by the report of Mr. William Nelson from the National Archives. By November 15, 1899, ten deceased U.S. soldiers were disinterred at Casper, and reinterred in the post cemetery at Fort D. A. Russell. W. I. Bonwell of Company F, Eleventh Kansas Cavalry, who was killed June 8, 1865, was moved from the original grave near Garden Creek five miles south of Casper to grave number 233 in Section C. Four unknown bodies of men of the Eleventh Kansas Cavalry who died in 1865 were removed from original graves near the North Platte River opposite old Fort Caspar and reburied in graves numbered 238, 239, and 240; the partial remains of two bodies which were found in one grave were reburied in grave number 240. An unknown soldier of the same regiment was removed from one mile south of old Fort Caspar to grave number 241.

The remains in grave 241 might be those of Private Edwin Summers, who was killed south of the river, or possibly of Private James Ballau, whose body was reported missing. The four men who were killed with Lieutenant Caspar Collins were probably among those removed to Fort Russell, but it is highly improbable that they included any of the men killed at the wagon-train fight. These men lie in an unmarked grave somewhere on Custard Hill.

of the Indians, who were soon ascertained to be in full retreat; then the detachment was ordered to the spot where the wagon train had put up such a gallant fight.[22]

On arriving there a horrible sight met our gaze. Twenty-one of our dead soldiers were lying on the ground, stripped naked and mangled in every conceivable way. I noticed one poor fellow with a wagon tire across his bowels and from appearances, it had been heated red hot and then laid upon him while still alive, so that the red devils might gloat over the torture they were inflicting before the breath of life had entirely left the body. From the appearance of the other bodies I believe he was the only one tortured, and therefore I believe he was the only one left alive at the time they captured the train. Every one of them was scalped, but the Indians had left the scalps lying around on the ground, which was a sure sign that their loss had been so heavy they did not think they had cause to exult over their victory. We counted about forty lodge pole trails on which they had fixed stretchers to carry off their wounded. We heard, some time after, that their loss was over 60 killed and about 130 badly wounded. The loss on our side was Lt. Collins and 27 men killed, eleven or twelve wounded, and one missing. We presumed the missing man was killed but we could not find his body. It may have been possible that the Indians captured him and carried him away to torture at one of their villages.

The command returned to the station, and the next morning we went out and buried our fellow heroes in the ground upon which they had so nobly, yet unavailingly, fought. The most of those who had been killed with the train belonged to Company H of the 11th Kansas, and it was always considered the best company in the regiment when there was any real fighting to be done, and yet, up to this time, the company had escaped with fewer fatalities than any other company in the regiment. It seemed so much harder to bear to think that after three years' fighting against the rebels they were ordered out on the plains to fight Indians, and now, when the orders were out for their return home, where they were to be mustered out, they were so ruthlessly slaughtered. We have the consolation of knowing that they died with their faces to the foe, and that in death, as in their three years' service, they sustained the proud reputation

22 Drew, *loc. cit.,* May 25, 1882.

gained by this regiment of always doing its duty, no matter what odds were pitted against them.[23]

Private S. H. Fairfield visited the wagon train site with another party:

On the afternoon of the 27th 25 of us boys, under Lt. Paul Grimm, went out in search of Sergeant Custard and his men. We followed the telegraph road among the hills. Several miles from the bridge we came to a washout, where the boys had made a stand.

On three sides the embankment was three or four feet high, but on the west there was only slight protection. Into this washout they had driven one of their wagons, and from behind such meagre embankment the poor fellows fought for their lives for five long hours. Here we found the mangled and mutilated bodies of Sergeant Custard and his 18 men. 17 of them had been left lying upon their faces, their bodies pinioned to the ground with long spears. They had been stripped and cut up in a shocking manner. The waggoner was strapped to his feed box, and hot irons from the hubs of the wagon wheels were placed along his back, apparently when he was alive. The charred remains of one man were among the coals where the wagon was burned. The next day another detail of 25 men under Lt. Hubbard, went out and buried the poor fellows where they had sacrificed their lives so dearly. A long ditch was dug and lined with blankets. In it the dead were laid side by side, with rubber blankets spread over them, and the bodies were covered with the sands of the desert. How many Indians were killed in the battle will never be known. In a communication from General Dodge, he says: "Information from our scouts show that their loss must have been greater than first supposed. The Indians threw away all of the scalps they had taken from our men, a sure sign that they had lost more than they had killed. It was estimated that over 2000 Indians were engaged in the fight, and that one-third of Major Anderson's forces were killed or wounded.[24]

Lieutenant Drew and Private Fairfield claim that their detachments first discovered the Custard site on July 27 and went

---

[23] *Ibid.*
[24] Fairfield, *loc. cit.*, 359–60.

back to bury the bodies on July 28.[25] Their accounts were written many years after the battle and are probably not correct in regard to dates. Sergeant Pennock was undoubtedly more accurate when he wrote in his Diary that the bodies were found on July 28 and buried on July 29:

> July 28, 1865: . . . No Indians appeared up to 2 o'clock P.M. A detachment started out to find our boys above. About five miles west from the station 20 dead bodies were found, the wagons burned. The Indians had a great many killed and wounded. They had to cut up a great many telegraph poles and split them to drag off their killed and wounded. The Indian scouts (Snake) say there were 3,000 Indians at least went north from the Trail the telegraph lines destroyed as far west as the party went about six to eight miles.
>
> July 29, 1865: Move back this A.M. from station to camp. A strong party went out to bury the dead. Twenty-one bodies were buried on the battle ground. A horrible sight. All scalped, but one, and bodies nearly all burned up. The savages set fire to the wagons and heated bolts and burned the men with them and turned their feet to the fire torturing them alive in every possible manner. They were buried in two graves. Seven in one thirteen in the other. One was buried on the other side of the river from where the train was taken. Wire cut east.[26]

The little wagon corral was found one and one-quarter miles straight across country from the post, or about two miles by road, 150 yards south of the telegraph road. The twenty men found dead and later buried there included the two teamsters, Private Rice B. Hamilton of Company I, Eleventh Ohio Cavalry, and Private Adam Culp, of Company I, Eleventh Kansas Cavalry, and eighteen men of Companies D and H, Eleventh Kansas Cavalry. The eleven dead of Company H were Commissary Sergeant Amos J. Custard and Privates Jesse E. Antram, William Brown, George Heil, August Hoppe, John Horton, William B. Long, Ferdinand Schafer, Samuel Sproul, Thomas W.

---

[25] *Ibid;* Drew, *loc. cit.,* May 25, 1882.
[26] Pennock, *loc. cit.,* 21.

Young, and William West. The seven dead of Company D were teamster Martin Green and Privates William D. Gray, William H. Miller, Thomas Powell, Samuel Tull, Jacob Zinn, and John R. Zinn.[27]

The soldier buried one mile south of the river was Private Edwin Summers, who had refused to go with the others and was last seen heading toward the foothills, closely pursued by several warriors.[28] Although the body of Private James Ballau, who had been shot on the riverbank, was never found, he was later officially listed in the muster rolls and reports as killed. Twenty-two soldiers of Sergeant Custard's detachment were listed as dead, together with Private James A Porter of Company I, who was killed with Lieutenant Walker's party. Four men of Companies H, I, and K, Eleventh Kansas Cavalry, had been killed with Lieutenant Collins, making a total of twenty-seven men killed during the hostilities of July 26. General Connor, in his report of July 27, said that there were twenty-five men of the Eleventh Kansas Cavalry killed, apparently excluding Private Hamilton of the Eleventh Ohio Cavalry and Private James Ballau, whose body had not been found.[29] At least ten men were in the post hospital severely wounded, but none of them died of their wounds.[30] Many had wounds which were less severe, while many horses had been killed and wounded. It is probable that none of the mules at the wagon train was killed, as no bones have been found in the vicinity.

[27] Muster rolls of Companies D, H, and I, Eleventh Kansas Cavalry, dated August 31, 1865, and of Company I, Eleventh Ohio Cavalry, dated August 31, 1865; Muster-out rolls of Companies D and H, Eleventh Kansas Cavalry.

[28] Mokler, *Fort Caspar*, 41. Corporal Shrader told Mr. Mokler that he buried Summers one mile south of the river, but in the reprint of the Oskaloosa *Independent*, in the *Capital*, July 3, 1882, it is reported that he was buried half a mile south of the river. As the river makes a sharp bend from south to north here, it is difficult to determine just where the place of burial could have been. Shrader was unable to find it during his trip of 1926.

[29] "Roster of Eleventh Cavalry Volunteer Regiment," *loc. cit.*

[30] *Ibid.* Mokler says there were eleven men in the hospital. Mokler, *Fort Caspar*, 49.

There is no way of knowing the exact number of casualties among the warriors. Even if we accept George Bent's statement that eight Cheyennes were killed, they were a small tribe, and as there were many tribes of Sioux and some Arapahoes there, it would seem that Lieutenant Drew's information that there were over 60 Indians killed and 130 wounded was not out of line. Lieutenant Walker reported that the ranchmen and scouts at Platte Bridge said that the Indian trail gave evidence of several hundred Indians' having been killed or badly wounded and hauled away on tipi poles.[31]

Details were gathered from the three men who escaped, from the evidences left on the ground, and from the Indians themselves, who told the squaw of a Frenchman named Redhan, whom they captured a few days after at Rock Creek, twenty miles below Fort Halleck, of their numbers, the time of the fight, of the terrible resistance, and their large excess of losses over that of the whites. . . . The mutilated bodies and fragments of bodies were gathered together and buried with military honors in one grave.[32]

It is possible that the valiant defense of the little wagon train saved Platte Station. The Indians had already sustained heavy losses that morning from Lieutenant Collins' men and from the Sioux's and Cheyennes' firing into each other. After suffering such severe casualties and wreaking their vengeance on Sergeant Custard's men, the war party lost its taste for further fighting and split up; most of the warriors returning to the Powder River country. However some of them went south and attacked wagon trains on the Overland route, while a band of two hundred Cheyennes followed along the mail road near the Laramie River, raiding the white settlements.[33] The popular estimates placing the

[31] Walker, *loc. cit.*, 339.
[32] "Military History of the Eleventh Kansas Volunteer Cavalry," *loc. cit.*, 213.
[33] "MAJOR J. W. BARNES,   August 7, 1865
    AAG Ft. Leavenworth
200 Cheyenne Indians attacked station near Big Laramie on 1st Inst. killed 4 men and 1 woman and took one 15 year old woman prisoner and 1 girl baby. Also made a break on Little Laramie stealing 13 Govt horses and losing 4 killed

number of warriors at twenty-five hundred to three thousand seem too high. General P. E. Connor was probably more accurate when he stated in his telegram of July 27 that one thousand hostile Indians attacked the station.[34]

On August 1 a telegram was received that the Sixth Michigan (one of Custer's old outfits) would arrive the next day, and the "joyful tick, tick, tick [of the telegraph key] put a glad smile on every countenance. . . . All is gladness and joy."[35] An advance guard of twenty-eight men of the Michigan troops arrived the next day, and on August 3 at 5:30 A.M. the Eleventh Kansas Cavalry was homeward bound.[36]

Sergeant Pennock's account of the return trip reads like a timetable of the old Oregon Trail. First came Horse Creek (three miles from the station), then Reshaw Creek (seven miles from the station), Deer Creek Station, and Big Muddy Creek, where camp was made the first night. The next day Boxelder Creek was crossed and camp made on La Prelle Creek. On August 5 they passed Bed-Tick Creek and Wagon Hound, camping at La Bonté Station. On Sunday, August 6, they struck the North Platte River, passing Horseshoe Station, Little Bitter Cottonwood and Big Bitter Cottonwood, and camped six miles west of Fort Laramie. As the men saw these landmarks for the last time, they must have reflected upon the parts they had played in the bloody scenes that had been enacted there.[37]

Upon reaching Fort Kearny on the last day of August, the soldiers turned in their horses and equipment. Arriving at Fort

---

all cavalry in pursuit. Indians supposed to be part of band that made fight at Platte Bridge few days ago.

GEORGE F. PRICE, CAPT. AND AAA GENERAL
(FOR CONNOR)

The War of the Rebellion, Series I, Vol 48, p. 357.

[34] Telegram dated July 27, 1865, from Brigadier General P. E. Connor to Major J. W. Barnes, assistant adjutant general, U. S. Serial Set [U. S. Congress], Serial 3436, *H.R. Doc. 369,* Pt 1, p. 357.

[35] Pennock, *loc. cit.,* 22.

[36] *Ibid.*

[37] *Ibid.,* 22–23.

PLATTE RIVER BRIDGE

From a pencil sketch made by a member of the Eleventh Kansas Cavalry who was there and participated in the fight, July 25-27, 1865.

Photograph by the author

Sergeant Custard found the telegraph patrol at the bend in the North Platte River at right. His supply train disappeared over the high ridge in the distance.

Photograph by the author

The wagon-train fight occurred in the hollow in the middle ground.

Leavenworth on September 11, they were discharged from the service of the United States on September 19,1865. The Eleventh Kansas Cavalry was home at last, but twenty-seven of their comrades had been left behind at the last minute, filling unmarked graves on the field of valor where they fell.

When Major General G. M. Dodge wrote to Colonel William O. Collins extending his condolences for the loss of his son, the grief-stricken father replied in a letter dated September 4, 1865, condemning Major Anderson for ordering his son to lead a small body of men in such a forlorn hope and requesting that there be an investigation of the conduct of the Major.[38] An investigation was held at Fort Laramie, and Major W. H. Evans of the Eleventh Ohio Cavalry made the report on April 7, 1866. Major Anderson was condemned for failing to send relief to the wagon train under cover of darkness, for ordering Lieutenant Collins to lead the relief party when it should have been led by the Kansas line officers who were present and able to lead it, and for not recalling Lieutenant Collins and his party when he was being surrounded.[39] The investigation was carried on by officers of the rival Eleventh Ohio Cavalry, and none of the participants in the action was present.

While it seems difficult to justify Major Anderson's ordering Lieutenant Collins to head the relief party when there were Kansas line officers present, the answer might be found in the report of Major General Dodge, which stated that the men were "mutinous—demand their discharge."[40] The probabilities are that he did try to get them to go, but that they gave various excuses, and he took the easy way out by commanding Lieutenant Collins to lead the detachment, which he had a right to do.

The other two charges seem to be groundless. If Lieutenant Bretney had gone to the relief of Sergeant Custard shortly after

[38] Mokler, *Fort Caspar*, 51–52.
[39] *Ibid.*, 46–48.
[40] *The War of the Rebellion*, Series II, Vol. 48, p. 1132.

he arrived at the post at two o'clock, he would not have met him until broad daylight, and the total military force of the garrison, being divided into two parts and widely separated, would have been especially vulnerable to the massed Indian attacks. Judging from all the eyewitness accounts it was not necessary to recall Lieutenant Collins, because he started to charge back to the bridge as soon as he saw Indians approaching him from all sides. It should be borne in mind that the horses at the post were not in very good condition, as is attested by the fact that Lieutenant Walker could find only seventeen serviceable horses when he started out that morning to repair the telegraph line.

Lieutenant Drew was probably right when he said, "At that time we thought the Major too cautious but since then, knowing what the Indians did to Fetterman's party the next year near Fort Phil Kearny, and later to the gallant Custer and his brave men at Little Big Horn, we are satisfied that the Major's decision was a wise one, and that by it alone are any of us left alive today."[41]

Back near Big Springs, Kansas, Thomas Custard, age nine years, and Flora Anna Custard, age eight years, were living with their aunt, Salome Geelan, when the news came that their father had been killed. Their Uncle George came to Big Springs to

[41] Drew, *loc. cit.*, May 18, 1882.

William Young Drew was born in New York City on March 7, 1834, and came to Kansas with his father, John Drew, and brother Josiah in 1855. He served as first lieutenant in Company I, Eleventh Kansas Cavalry, under Captain James E. Greer, but was mustered out in September, 1865, with the rank of captain. He was married to Martha Helen Promeroy on September 24, 1863, in Burlingame, Kansas, by the Rev. Jerard W. Fox, and their marriage was the first to be recorded in the county. Six children were born of their marriage, of whom Mabel Drew Thorburn and Ethel Drew Truitt are still living and have graciously furnished this sketch of their father's life. After the war Drew carried on a very lucrative lumber and contracting business in Burlingame and Osage City until 1877. From 1870 to 1886 he held various government positions about the state but maintained his residence in Burlingame. After living in Topeka for three years, he returned to Burlingame, where he was cashier in the First National Bank. He retired in 1903, moving to Riverside, California, and died on August 16, 1904, at the age of seventy.

take them back to Pennsylvania, where they then lived with Amos' mother. Later Thomas returned and farmed the old homestead. Anna married William Mossinger in 1903. When her husband died in 1919, Thomas went to Pennsylvania to visit her. After selling her interest in the estate, the west eighty acres, she lived in a little four-room house in Pennsylvania until 1934, when she sold it and entered an old ladies' home, where she died in 1943, leaving no children. Thomas married Louise Facer in 1881 and served as justice of the peace and on the local school board. His oldest daughter, Ethel, married William Warner, by whom she had a son and daughter. A son, Charles James Custard, and a younger daughter, Elsie Price, are still living. Thomas Custard died in 1928.

After he had been mustered out, James W. Shrader returned to the farm where his parents lived, near Oskaloosa, grateful that he had been spared in the terrible ordeal. In 1867 he married Lauretta Conwell, and they lived on a farm near Oskaloosa until 1908 when he sold it and moved to a thirty-three-acre tract at the edge of town. When too old to take care of the tract, he sold the land, retaining the house and some vacant lots. Shrader and his wife had three children who lived to maturity, one other dying in infancy. Their eldest son, William Wallace Shrader, was married to Lena Bliss from Ohio on February 22, 1903. Three children were born to this marriage, only one of whom, Mary Douglas, now survives. James Shrader's eldest daughter, Cora Catherine Shrader, was married to Carl Snyder but left no children. The youngest daughter, Victoria Shrader, born in 1882, still lives in Topeka, Kansas. Lauretta Conwell Shrader passed away in 1917, while James W. Shrader, sometime corporal in the Eleventh Kansas Cavalry, joined the "innumerable caravan" in 1929.

10

Search and Research

AFTER THE VALIANT STRUGGLE of Sergeant Custard's little band, the charred skeletons of the wagons remained beside the telegraph road where they had been burned. The one on the south rim of the hollow may have rolled down over the side of the bluff; Marion N. Wheeler of Casper, Wyoming, an early resident in the area, says that as a boy, in 1904, he saw heavy-duty iron from a heavy wagon of the army type, including a wagon tire about two and one-half inches wide and one-half inch thick, a hub, wooden spindle, and other iron and wooden wagon parts, at the foot of the bluff south of the battle site. One might speculate that when the wagon was burned, the brake was released or that the Indians may have given it the little push it needed to send the flaming mass down the slope. The remaining wagons eventually disappeared. The emigrants, soldiers, and supply trains which were continually passing by on this branch of the Oregon Trail may have dismantled them in order to obtain the spare wagon parts. Early-day ranchers used the scrap iron in their blacksmith shops.[1] In a few years nothing was left to mark the site, and with the passage of time the exact place was lost.

Aware of their rich heritage, in 1936 the citizens of Casper,

[1] Oral statements by Mark J. Davis and Marion N. Wheeler, old-time residents of the area, to the author in the summer of 1959.

as a community project, rebuilt old Fort Casper with logs on the actual site of the old buildings and established a museum there. The reconstruction is completely accurate except that many of the original buildings were built of adobe and the old stockade has not been reconstructed. Two architects contributed their services and, after obtaining scale copies of the army plans and specifications of the post, dug down to the charred foundations and built on the actual ruins of the old fort. When the course of the river shifted to the north at this point, the old piers of the bridge and the rock-filled cribs on which it rested were on dry land. Workmen uncovered many tons of rock from the cribs and two thousand iron spikes, some twenty inches long and one inch thick, which had held the logs together to form the cribbing. Old timbers were excavated from the piers, so there can be no question that this is the exact location of the old Guinard bridge.[2] Visitors today can walk along the row of mounds which supported the bridge and in mind's eye see the heavily laden wagons, emigrant families, soldiers, and Indians as they passed over it a century before.

Historically minded residents of the area have tried without success to find the battlefield where Custard's men were killed, searching from the present restoration of Fort Casper to the saddle gap four miles to the west. On July 26, 1931, the Natrona County Historical Society, under the leadership of Robert S. Ellison, dedicated with appropriate ceremony twenty-one marble monoliths, which were placed in a little swale three miles west of the fort in honor of the soldiers who supposedly fell at or near that place. A monument, with an inscription furnished by the

[2] Mokler, *Fort Caspar,* 60–65; Oral statements (summer 1959), to author by Leon Goodrich, one of the architects of the reconstructed fort. That the reconstruction is actually on the site of the old fort is verified by Marion N. Wheeler in his letters to the author dated June 29, 1962, and July 20, 1962. In 1904, Mr. Wheeler, as a boy of high-school age, rode into Casper many times past the fort and could still see the old iron pile at the station blacksmith shop. The parade ground was located east and south of the little cemetery, on ground now covered by the western portion of the fair grounds.

army, was also placed on a little knoll several hundred yards southwest of the markers in commemoration of the "Red Buttes Fight," referring to the Custard wagon-train fight.[3] In so designating the engagement, they followed the wording of some early reports, although the Red Buttes are fully ten miles southwest of the actual place and out of sight of it. It has been suggested that it was called the "Red Buttes Fight" in the early days in order to convey the impression that the fort was too far away to send aid to the beleaguered wagon train. Whatever may have been the reason, the name is a misnomer and definitely misleading. Mr. Ellison and the Society are to be commended upon their patriotic zeal, but the monument and markers are over a mile from the spot where the action occurred.

At the time the markers were dedicated, the site and name were vigorously protested by the eminent author and historian of Casper, the late Alfred James Mokler. After extensive investigation he had concluded that the place of the fight was three-quarters of a mile south of the Ellison site, on a hill south of the telegraph road and about three miles west of Fort Casper. He reasoned from the accounts that Custard came over the saddle gap and, upon seeing the Indians, made a dash for the fort but got only about one mile before he had to corral. However, this site is also out of sight of the fort. Both Mr. Ellison and Mr. Mokler spent years looking for the Custard site; if they had had the aid of modern electronic devices, they would undoubtedly have found it long ago.

When Corporal Shrader was in Casper in the summer of 1926, he attempted to locate the place where Custard and his men were killed, but the country had changed so much during sixty-one years that he was unable to recognize the old landmarks or to say where the men were buried. The ridges and hills were not as high and the valleys were not as deep. He could not even find the grave of Private Edwin Summers, whose body he claimed

[3] Mokler, *Fort Caspar*, 73–74.

to have buried one mile south of the river. He said that while he was digging the grave for Summers, he could plainly see the twenty-five men in the command of Lieutenant Hubbard on the hill on the north side of the river, digging a trench for the burial of the men at the wagon-train site. He also said that he had looked along the riverbank for the body of Ballau, but could not find it and supposed that it had either floated down the river or that the Indians had taken it.[4]

John C. Friend, who had been a telegraph operator at Sweetwater Station but was present at Platte Bridge as a private in Company G, Eleventh Ohio Cavalry, during the fight, attended the dedication ceremony of the Oregon Trail–Caspar Collins marker on July 5, 1920. At that time he said that the exact spot where the body of Lieutenant Caspar Collins was found was unknown but was from two to four miles north of the bridge. The terrain had changed and the old landmarks were gone. When the party went out to bring in the dead, the men spread out in a fan shape to go over the hills. After an hour one of the party, who had gone in a northerly direction from the marker, signaled that the body had been found. A box was made and lined with blankets. The body was placed in the box and buried in the post cemetery on the south side of the river east of the station.[5]

While she was state historian of Wyoming, Agnes Wright Spring, doing extensive research on the Platte Bridge fight and the personal life of Lieutenant Caspar Collins, obtained much information from Captain Henry C. Bretney, then a resident of Jacksonville, Florida, and John C. Friend, having the benefit of the research of Robert S. Ellison. Her book, *Caspar Collins*, is recognized as authoritative for the life of the unfortunate young lieutenant.

After forty years of research, Alfred James Mokler, late of Casper, Wyoming, wrote *Fort Caspar*. Through the courtesy

[4] *Ibid.*, 43–44.
[5] *Ibid.*, 69–70.

of Henry C. Bretney, of Jacksonville, Florida, a son of the Captain Bretney mentioned above, he had access to the material left by the deceased Captain Bretney. He also obtained firsthand information from John C. Friend and Corporal James W. Shrader, who had taken part in the battle. This excellent book contains a factual analysis of the engagement and a history of the local memorials.

A mild controversy developed when an article entitled "The Platte Bridge Battle" appeared in the Topeka *Daily Capital* for April 16, 1882, over the name of "An Army Officer." The same article was printed years later as "Old Fort Casper" in the *Wyoming Historical Collections*, under the name of Charles Whitehead, who was presumably a member of the telegraph patrol at Red Buttes when Sergeant Custard passed. It came to the attention of Willam Y. Drew, who lived in Burlingame, Kansas. Noting that there were many inaccuracies in the account, Drew wrote his verison of the battle in an article entitled "Platte Bridge Fight," published serially in the Osage County *Chronicle* (April 20, 27, May 11, 18, and 25, 1882.) An unknown writer on the Oskaloosa *Independent* was prompted to write an account of the part played by Corporal Shrader's little band, which was reprinted in the Topeka *Daily Capital* on July 3, 1882. In September, 1918, while passing through Casper, Colonel W. W. Denison, then adjutant general of the state of Kansas, who had been at Platte Bridge during the battle as a private in Company I, submitted during an interview with the press the article of William Y. Drew, which was printed serially in the Casper *Tribune* on September 10, 11, 12, and 13, 1918. As Colonel Denison submitted the article without criticism or correction, it may be assumed that he agreed with Drew.

In the spring of 1958, L. C. Bishop of Cheyenne, Wyoming, and the writer, after reading all known accounts to date of the Custard wagon-train fight, determined to find the location with the aid of a metal detector. Where five wagons were burned, there must have been metal wagon parts and other debris scattered around. Of the three main branches of the Oregon Trail west of Casper, Mr. Bishop had already found that the one on the bluffs next to the river on the north side was the telegraph road. Most of the accounts placed the site at from three to six miles west of the post, and a map drawn by Lieutenant Walker in later years showed the place six miles west of it. Since Lieutenant Walker did not accompany the burial parties, his map placing the site in a deep valley out of sight of the post was obviously incorrect. Bearing in mind that the location was in plain sight of the fort, Mr. Bishop and I started at the saddle gap and worked down the telegraph road and along the south side of it. As the view from this location is very deceptive, we did not notice at the time that the fort could not be seen from here, being cut off by an intervening ridge jutting southward towards the river. Since a painting by the western artist, William H. Jackson, showed the little corral south of the road and nearly a mile down from the saddle gap, where Mr. Mokler claimed it was, we covered all this area thoroughly for four days, finding nothing but the usual broken horseshoes and bits of iron.

Deciding that the site must be closer to the fort, we came back later and spent three days going over the north branch of the telegraph road from the place where it comes over the ridge south of the Poison Spider Road, on towards Casper. We found only an old grave on a little hill south of the road. Although all were out of sight of the post, we went over the present monument and markers situated on the north branch, where Ellison claimed the engagement took place, and found nothing. Later I spent several days going down the north branch of the road from the saddle gap to the monument, but without result. We also spent considerable time along an old trail running south of the telegraph road along some lower bluffs and then on the flat along the river. This was the easy road, which Sergeant Custard did not take, fearing an ambush.

In the middle of June I stopped in Casper for three days to make a final effort. Deciding to start at the other end and recalling the words of Private S. H. Fairfield, "We followed the telegraph road among the hills," I started westward along the ruts about a quarter of a mile north of the W. G. Boles residence and ascended the bluffs, looking for the little hollow south of it. When nothing was found the first trip, another attempt was made, during which the edge of the bluffs above the river was explored. Finally, at the end of the third day, I made one more trip up the telegraph road and circled around in a hollow on the eastern slope of a little hill. On the south side of the hollow I finally got a buzz from the detector and found a number of musket balls in the bottom of an old handmade water jug, buried about six inches deep. Near them were some handmade wagon bolts and parts of wagons which had been burned.

We made many more trips to the site, making a complete coverage of the area with the metal detector. There were no cartridge cases to be found here: in those days the Indians did not yet have the Henry and Spencer rifles using metallic cartridges, and the Smith cartridges of the soldiers left only a small piece of foil a little over an inch square after firing. Besides burned wagon parts we found one of the cartridge foils and three flattened-out and curved lead musket balls which had apparently struck the iron tires of the wagon in the corral facing south. A bullet fired from a navy Colt .36 was also found close to the road. There was nothing above ground, everything being buried from two to eight inches deep.

By far the largest concentration of burned handmade wagon parts and the three flattened-out musket balls were found around the place where the original discovery was made, and we labeled that site "A." Two burned wagon bolts and nuts were found sixty feet south of the location of the musket balls, indicating that another wagon was farther up the slope. In our opinion this was where two or three wagons were corralled and where the main fighting took place. The sagebrush was sparse here for an area about fifty yards in diameter, which might have been burned out when the wagons were burned.

The following is a list of articles found at site A within a radius of sixty feet of the place where the musket balls in the water jug were found:

20 .503 and .546 lead balls (none of which had been fired)
 6 small pieces of hoops (probably from a nail keg or water bucket)
 1 small metal buckle (probably used in back of trousers)
 2 4d cut nails
 1 small metal button from clothing
 1 small piece of lead, possibly lead foil from cartridge
12 pieces of crockery from handmade water jug
 3 harness rings 1½" and 2" in diameter
 3 lead balls that have been flattened by striking iron
 1 ⅜-inch x 4-inch bolt with square shank and round head(probably from a wagon)
 1 staple from hame of a harness
 1 large buckle (probably from a halter)
 1 small buckle (probably used in back of trousers)
 1 10d cut nail
 1 ½-inch nut
 1 ⅜-inch nut
 1 heavy ½-inch washer
 1 ¾-inch x 3-inch strip of iron with large rivet (probably from a wagon box)
 1 flat-head screw 1 inch long (probably from a feed box)
 1 strip of iron 1 inch x 8 inches with two holes (probably from a wagon box)
 1 cast iron handle 11 inches long (probably from lead melting pot or frying pan)
 3 ⅜-inch iron nut
 1 candleholder for 1¼-inch candle, with sharp handle
 1 bale clip from wooden bucket
 1 repair chain link which had been pulled open

One hundred and forty yards north of site A just south of the road were found more wagon parts; this place we called site "B." The articles found within a radius of thirty feet of this point were as follows:

1 piece of iron ⅜ inch x 4 inches x 1½ inches with four notches from wagon brake assembly
2 pieces of iron hinge (probably from cover of feed box on a wagon)
1 piece of iron thimble from wagon hub
1 piece of zinc or heavy tin
1 piece of hoop (probably from a water bucket)
2 1¼-inch wood screws with ends broken or burned off
1 small piece of tin
1 .36 caliber bullet which had been fired from navy Colt cap-and-ball revolver
1 circular piece of heavy wire used for holding telegraph wire to wood-covered insulators
1 piece of ⅜-inch iron rod
1 ⅝-inch iron rod 4 inches long with ¾-inch eye at one end, hand hammered (probably from tail gate of a wagon)
1 small piece of tin
1 very old lard pail buried deep
1 strip of iron 1¼ inches x 4 inches (probably from wagon box)

According to this evidence a wagon was undoubtedly burned at site B, so far from site A that it was probably not in the corral —very likely it was abandoned by the men after the first sudden attack. All of the iron and steel items listed at sites A and B had been burned. One hundred yards east of site B and near the trail we found a glass insulator from the old telegraph line.

Fifty yards east of site B and upon the ruts of the old road we found two pieces of ½-inch cast iron from the thimble of a wagon hub and four pieces of tin, all of which had been burned. This was called site "C." Sixty yards farther east on the road were two pieces of ¼-inch cast iron from the thimble of a wagon hub, five pieces of tin, one piece of spring steel 2 inches x ⅝ inch x 1/32 inch thick, and two small pieces of tin ½ inch wide with

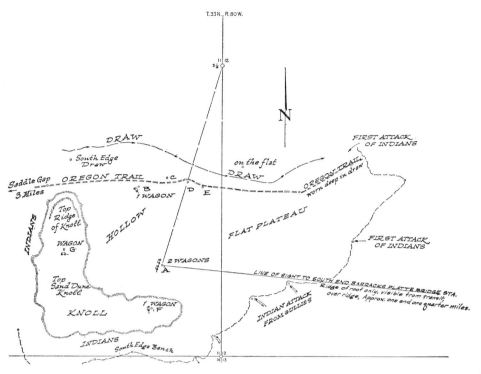

Site of the Wagon-Train Fight

holes on one side and small notches on the other. All had been burned, and the site was labeled "D."

Site E was located sixty yards east of site D where one broken handmade iron chain link ¾-inch iron, one handmade iron pin ¾ inch in diameter sloping to ½ inch and 9 inches long, one curved piece of thin cast iron, probably from a lead melting pot, one small piece of melted lead or solder, one ⅜-inch iron washer, and one piece lead foil from a .50-caliber Smith carbine were found. In order to identify this last item, we purchased from Phillip Jay Medicus of New York City, a well-known authority on antique firearms, a .50-caliber Smith cartridge manufactured during the Civil War, and the size and folds in the lead foil covering were identical with those of the one found here. As sites C, D, and E were on the road and out of sight of the fort, we concluded that the parts found there had probably fallen from a wagon while it was being towed away.

In making a complete coverage of the area, we found sixty yards southwest of site A, up on the rim of the hollow, one ⅜-inch iron nut, one 1-inch wagon wrench with handle broken off, and one large iron staple, all of which had been burned. This was called site F. We concluded that the lead wagon had stopped here and later rolled down the slope and over the bluffs.

Mark J. Davis of Casper, Wyoming, told me that he had been advised by some early residents that one burned wagon stood for several years on the north end of the hill. I found a burned and badly worn mule shoe here and labeled this site "G." It is surmised that when firing was heard, the teamster of the rear wagon tried to cut across the hill in an attempt to join the wagons in the hollow but had to abandon the attempt when the Indians charged.

It is possible but unlikely that the corral was composed of wagons at each of the seven sites located and spread in a semicircle over an area about two hundred yards in diameter and that there was fighting from all of the wagons. Since there were only twenty men with the train, the natural tendency would have been for them to concentrate behind a few wagons close together in the shelter of the hollow. This is borne out by the fact that most of the relics were found at site A, where at least two wagons and possibly more, were together.

Everything was found on the land of W. G. Boles definitely located in the SE¼ of the SE¼ of Section 11, Township 33 North Range 80, in Natrona County, Wyoming. The burned wagon parts have been examined by old-timers, who have all pronounced them genuine and handmade, dating back to 1865. The surprising scarcity of metal found is probably due to the removal of metal parts by emigrants and supply trains along the road or by early settlers, as was surmised earlier. Blowing sands over the years may have covered some too deep to be found. It is significant that we failed to find anything after a careful search of all the other possible sites between the Boles house and the saddle gap to the west. Had there been anything else in this area, we would have found it.

That this was the actual site of the wagon-train fight is confirmed by Mark J. Davis, a son of H. W. Davis, who came to the area in 1879. Mr. Davis, in August, 1959, offered to take me to the place and drove right to the Custard hill, approaching it from the northwest. He said that an old buffalo hunter, Boney Earnest, coming along the old road a year after the battle, had seen the burned wagons standing along the road in plain sight, one of them on the north end of the crest of the hill. Jim Smith, a freighter in the early days, saw all the wagons and debris a few years later. Both men showed Mr. Davis the place in about 1923. It was a common practice for the settlers in the area to get their iron scrap from the wagons for use in their blacksmith shops. Mr. Davis also said that the river bend at the foot of the bluffs half a mile southwest of the place was a popular camping ground and that Custard may have stopped there to water his stock. It is doubtful that he stopped there, however, because in order to return to the road which he took over the bluffs, he would have had to go back half a mile west to the fork where he had turned off or take a very steep grade up to the bluffs. There is, however, strong evidence that the wagon train stopped to water the mules just before the attack.[6]

Looking westward from the fort, the saddle gap four miles away is not visible, being cut off from view by intervening bluffs which extend southward from the wagon-train site. The little ridge which Custard came over forms the sky line. Shrader's men were plainly seen from the fort when they crossed the river, which was possible only if they crossed in the vicinity of the Custard site. If they had crossed the river west of the ridge which the wagon train came over, they would not have been visible from the fort.

The bodies of the twenty men have not been located, although a power shovel generously furnished by the Natrona County Commissioners has been used in searching for them. A human radius from a forearm was found eight inches deep and six feet northwest of the unfired musket balls at site A, and part of a human toe bone was discovered on the road. The winds of ninety-five years have swept over these sand hills and may have buried the bodies too deep to be found.[7] Perhaps this is just as well. The proud veterans who fought here would be humiliated to have their burned and broken remains exposed to the public view a century after their brave struggle.

The soldiers from Platte Station fittingly named this place "Custard's Hill" in honor of the gallant sergeant.[8] The valiant stand made here by this little band of heroes ranks in the annals

---

[6] Grinnell, *op. cit.*, 224.

[7] The army has no record of the interment of Custard's men or of the removal of the remains from the original burial place (letter dated November 3, 1958, from John J. Flynn, lieutentant colonel, QMC, chief, Cemetery Branch, Memorial Division, Office of Quartermaster General, to the author).

[8] Mokler, *Fort Caspar*, 44.

of warfare with the Alamo, the Little Big Horn, and other battles where a few men were wiped out by overwhelming numbers.

In order to complete our research, Mr. Bishop and I decided to go to the site of the old Sweetwater Station and drive back to Casper over the Oregon Trail, which Sergeant Custard had followed. We drove westward on the highway about sixty miles to Independence Rock, also called the "Register of the Desert," which was one of the landmarks on the old road. This is a large mound of granite, rounded on the top, along the south base of which flows the Sweetwater River. Many emigrants who passed by in the early days carved their names and the dates on the rock, which is 1,950 feet long, 850 feet wide, 175 feet high, and 27 acres in area.[9] Here the road branches toward the west, but there is only the one road leading from here eastward to the vicinity of Emigrant Gap. Sweetwater Station was located one mile southeast of the rock on the bank of the Sweetwater River. There is nothing left of the station except excavations where the buildings stood. We spent about an hour poking around the rubbish and debris which covered the ground and then drove southeast over the old trail that the little wagon train had followed nearly a century before.

The present dirt road does not cover the exact site of the Oregon Trail, but the old ruts, which are worn in some places five or six feet deep, are plainly discernible along the road, first on one side and then on the other. After passing Horse Creek, we followed down the long, winding hill to Willow Springs, where there is now a small farmhouse on the bank of the little spring. Farther on was a grassy meadow around another spring where Custard had made camp. Here was acted out the little drama in which Sergeant Custard had refused to push on with Lieutenant Bretney because his mules were too tired. After passing Red Buttes, the road dips down southward towards the river; along

[9] Mokler, *History of Natrona County,* 457.

here is the bend where the bold sergeant refused to stay with the telegraph patrol. The road then ascends for about a mile to the ridge where the wagon train had passed from view. We had been lucky so far in being able to follow along the old trail, but halfway up this ridge, still about eight miles from Casper, we encountered a deep irrigation ditch which was impassable.

We were not very much disappointed, because we had driven to the saddle gap four miles west of Casper from the other direction many times and had looked over the intervening four miles to the ridge where we were forced to turn back. The trip from Sweetwater Station was an experience we will never forget, as we had seen the old familiar landmarks which the Sergeant had seen and had, in spirit, ridden with the little wagon train to the end of the journey.

Bibliography

1. *Manuscripts* and *Archival Material*

Bent, George. Letters to George E. Hyde, Yale University Library, New Haven.

————. Letters to George E. Hyde, Denver Public Library, Denver.

"Kansas in the Civil War." Newspaper clippings, Kansas State Historical Society, Topeka.

"Kansas Scrap Book." Newspaper clippings, Kansas State Historical Society, Topeka.

Osage County (Kansas) clippings. Newspaper excerpts, Kansas State Historical Society, Topeka.

Pennock, Isaac B. Diary, Kansas State Historical Society, Topeka. All references in this work are taken from the printed version in the *Annals of Wyoming*. q. v. *Newspapers* and *Articles*.

Ricker, Eli S. Interviews, Nebraska State Historical Society, Lincoln.

2. *Government Documents* and *Publications*

Muster Roll, Company D, Eleventh Kansas Cavalry, August 31,1865; Company H, Eleventh Kansas Cavalry, August 31, 1865; Company I, Eleventh Kansas Cavalry, August 31, 1865; Company K, Eleventh Kansas Cavalry, August 31, 1865; Company I, Eleventh Ohio Cavalry, August 31, 1865. National Archives, Old Army Branch, Washington.

Muster-out Roll, Company D, Eleventh Kansas Cavalry, September 13, 1865; Company H, Eleventh Kansas Cavalry, September 13, 1865. National Archives, Old Army Branch, Washington.

Report of the Adjutant General of the State of Kansas 1861–1865, Topeka, Reprint, ed., 1896.

Revised U.S. Army Regulations of 1861. (1863 ed.)

U. S. Serial Set (U.S. Congress), Serial 3436, *H.R. Doc. 369,* Pt. 1.

U. S. Serial Set (U.S. Congress), Serial 3437, *H.R. Doc. 369,* Pt. 2.

The War of the Rebellion: A Compilation of the Official Records of the Union and Confederate Armies, Series I, Vol. 48.

The War of the Rebellion: A Compilation of the Official Records of the Union and Confederate Armies, Series II, Vol. 48.

3. Books

Andreas, Alfred T. *History of the State of Kansas.* Chicago, A. T. Andreas, 1883.

Bartlett, I. S. *History of Wyoming.* 3 vols. Chicago, S. J. Clark Publishing Company, 1918.

Connelley, William E. *The Life of Preston B. Plumb.* Chicago, Browne and Howell, 1913.

Coutant, C. G. *The History of Wyoming.* Laramie, Chaplin, Safford and Mathison, 1899.

David, Robert B. *Finn Burnett, Frontiersman.* Glendale, Arthur H. Clark, 1937.

Gluckman, Acadi. *United States Muskets, Rifles, and Carbines.* Buffalo, Otto Ulbrich Co., Inc., 1948.

Grinnell, George Bird. *The Fighting Cheyennes.* New York, Charles Scribner's Sons, 1915. Norman, University of Oklahoma Press, 1956 (reprint). All references in this book are to the latter edition.

Hafen, L. R., and F. M. Young. *Fort Laramie and the Pageant of the West.* Glendale, Arthur H. Clark, 1938.

Hebard, C. R., and E. A. Brininstool. *The Bozeman Trail.* 2 vols. Cleveland, Arthur H. Clark, 1922.

Hyde, George E. *Red Cloud's Folk.* Norman, University of Oklahoma Press, 1957.

Lowe, Percival G. *Five Years a Dragoon ('49 to '54) and Other Adventures on the Great Plains.* Kansas City, F. Hudson Publishing Co., 1906.

Mokler, Alfred James. *Fort Caspar.* Casper, Prairie Publishing Co., 1939.

———. *History of Natrona County, Wyoming, 1888–1922.* Chicago, R. R. Donnelley & Sons Co., 1923.

Bibliography

————. *Transition of the West*. Chicago, R. R. Donnelley & Sons Co., 1927.

Riley, Harvey. *The Mule*. New York, Dick and Fitzgerald, 1867.

Spring, Agnes Wright. *Caspar Collins*. New York, Columbia University Press, 1927.

Trenholm, V. C. *Wyoming Pageant*. Casper, Prairie Publishing Company, 1946.

4. *Newspapers* and *Articles*

The Capital (Topeka), April 16, 1882; July 3, 1882.

Chronicle (Osage County), April 20, 27, May 11, 18, and 25, 1882.

Daily Conservative (Leavenworth), July 29, 1865.

The Daily Times (Leavenworth), August 19, 1865; August 30, 1865.

Democrat (Riley County), August 26, 1909.

Eagle (Wichita), November 1, 1931.

Robert Ellison, "The Platte Bridge Fight," *Winners of the West*, Vol. III (March 15, 1926).

Ferdinand Erhardt, "At Platte Bridge," *Kansas Scrap Book Biography E*, Vol. II, reprinted from *The National Tribune*, July 11, 1918.

S. H. Fairfield, "The Eleventh Kansas Regiment at Platte Bridge," *Kansas Historical Collections*, Vol. XIII, Topeka, 1904.

"Henry Lord of Dodge City Tells of the Battle of Platte Bridge," *Indian Depredations and Battles*, clippings, Vol. III, from Emporia (Kansas) *Gazette*, August 9, 1934.

Isaac B. Pennock, "Diary," *Annals of Wyoming*, Vol. XXIII (July, 1951).

Report of interview with J. W. Shrader in Atchison (Kansas) *Globe* reprinted in *Winners of the West*, Vol. III (May, 1926).

Tribune (Lawrence), July 29, 1865; August 3, 1865.

Tribune Herald (Casper), July 27, 1931; September 10, 11, 12, and 13, 1918.

George M. Walker, "Eleventh Kansas Cavalry, 1865, and the Battle of Platte Bridge," *Kansas Historical Collections*, Vol. XIV, Topeka, 1918.

Charles Whitehead, "Old Fort Casper," *Wyoming Historical Collections*, edited by R. C. Morris. Cheyenne, Sun-Leader Publishing House, 1897.

123

Index

130

THE BATTLE OF PLATTE BRIDGE

has been planned for maximum comfort in reading and handling. The type is eleven-point Old Style Number Seven, set on the Linotype with two points of spacing between lines. This face is transitional and has more "modern" than "old style" characteristics. As a letter form, it is without pretension or notable distinction, but its pragmatic sanction has always been its excellent readability for people in all walks of life.

UNIVERSITY OF OKLAHOMA PRESS

NORMAN